An Illustrated History of
WEST COUNTRY
CHINA CLAY TRAINS

Frontispiece: On 19th April 1985, No. 37207 *William Cookworthy,* the flagship of the china clay locomotive fleet, with its 'Cornish Railways' insignia on the yellow front end, approaches Middleway Bridge Crossing on the Newquay branch with two loaded 'Tiger' wagons from Goonbarrow Junction. They will be incorporated in the afternoons 'Speedlink' service to Severn Tunnel Junction.

J. Vaughan

Plate 1: A modern china clay train crosses the impressive Moorswater Viaduct, some 150ft. above the valley floor, on 21st November 1983. Seen through a 200mm Nikkor lens, 'Peak' Class 45/0 No. 45060 *Sherwood Forester* hauls the 09.15 St. Blazey to Severn Tunnel Junction formed of three 80 tonne (gross) 'Tiger' wagons and a 32 tonne slurry tanker towards Liskeard. The present viaduct dates back to 1881 and two piers of the original wooden topped 1859 viaduct can be seen on the left.

J. Vaughan

Plate 2 (Right): A typical china clay train comprising an 0-6-0PT locomotive and a rake of small wooden-sided 4-wheeled wagons. Although this photograph was taken on 23rd August 1961, it could have been taken at any time in the preceding 30 years. No. 4679 approaches Tavistock Junction, Plymouth with a load of china clay from the Marsh Mills Works. This section of track was shared with passenger trains working the service to Launceston but this was withdrawn from 31st December 1962.

R. C. Riley

An Illustrated History of WEST COUNTRY CHINA CLAY TRAINS

John Vaughan

Oxford Publishing Company

Plate 3: A quite outrageous shot of a very short china clay train. On 1st March 1984, a 117 tonne, 100m.p.h. express passenger locomotive in the shape of Class 50 No. 50018 *Resolution* was photographed heading up the valley of the River Fowey, north of Lostwithiel, with two 'Clay Hoods'. The locomotive was returning to Plymouth's Laira Depot but the destination of the clay wagons was not determined.

J. Vaughan

ISBN 0-86093-299-0

Typesetting by:
Colin Powell Typesetting & Design, Bournemouth, Dorset.

Printed in Great Britain by:
Biddles Ltd., Guildford, Surrey.

Published by:
Oxford Publishing Co.
Link House
West Street
POOLE, Dorset

INTRODUCTION

The history and operation of china clay trains has traditionally been a rather esoteric subject. Most railway enthusiasts know that china clay is a white substance and that it comes from the West Country, but generally little information about its transportation is available. There are many reference books which give a sentence or two on the subject and photographs of china clay trains are not uncommon. However, this is the first attempt to collate much of the available information in a single product. Although history is by no means overlooked, this volume is essentially pictorial and the overall balance leans towards modern times; a period when there has been the greatest change in the industry and in the trains which serve it.

The discovery of china clay in substantial volumes in the United Kingdom goes back about 240 years when the renowned William Cookworthy made discoveries near Helston, but later and more significantly near St. Austell in Cornwall. In this book I have outlined the early transportation problems and how some of the lessons learned from other Cornish mining activities were applied to the clay industry. From the early years of the 19th century china clay was transported on tramways, and these gradually developed into light railways and branch lines. Once the Cornish main line opened in 1859 and the ports of Par and Fowey were developed, china clay became an important revenue earner for the railways. Nearly all the china clay lines are featured in this volume and I have attempted to show something of the magnificent Cornish countryside, as well as the clay trains themselves. In addition to the railway lines of the South West there are sections showing china clay on the move from Menheniot to Markinch and from Beinn Dorain to Dover.

In the early days the staple motive power for china clay trains was the horse and I have included a photograph of a triple headed working. Gradually the steam engine was introduced and some interesting types of locomotives worked many of the minor lines. However, once the GWR and the L&SWR took over most of the lines, the motive power scene barely changed in over 70 years, although older classes of tank engine were replaced by similar but younger steam locomotives. Nearly 30 years ago the diesel locomotive arrived on the Cornish railway scene and diesel hydraulics finally replaced steam locomotives in 1964. All these early diesel classes are now extinct and even some of the later diesel electric classes have disappeared from BR. Over 15 classes of diesel locomotive are featured within and over 10 types of steam locomotive are illustrated. The basic concept of the 4-wheeled wooded sided china clay wagon has changed little over the years and indeed even in the mid-1980s about 400 of these little 12.5 tonners are still in use for short runs to the clay port of Fowey. However, especially since 1982 there have been significant freight rolling stock changes and most of the modern air-braked wagons are featured, including the variety of tankers which date back nearly 20 years to the early days of handling china clay slurry by rail.

This volume could not possibly have been prepared without the very valuable assistance of the English China Clay International Company. ECC could not have been more helpful in making information and illustrations available and Martin Pearce, Ivor Bowditch and Richard Fuller of ECC gave many hours of their valuable time in assisting the author with research and replying to many obscure questions about china clay trains and distribution. English China Clays Ltd. was incorporated in 1919 to acquire the assets of three major clay companies. During the next 66 years ECC acquired over 100 other companies to become the largest producer of china clay in the world, with a capacity of over three million tonnes per year. The group has international operations and in the County of Cornwall employs over 5,000 staff. The parent holding company is English China Clays PLC, the production company in the South West was English Clays Lovering Pochin and Co. Ltd. (ECLP) and the selling company which markets the clay products to customers in more than 60 countries and now the name used for all china clay activities is ECC International. Other china clay producing companies exist but most of the works and depots featured within this volume are managed by ECC and all the china clay in its various forms carried by the trains featured in the photographs is the product of either ECC or the Goonvean and Restowrack Clay Co. The Group is very aware of its position in the Cornish (and Devon) communities and it spends millions of pounds on the environment, seeding down old waste tips and screening and landscaping its mining and quarrying operations. Most of the china clay produced is transported by pipeline, road and ship but over ¾ million tonnes of clay is moved by BR every year and ECC makes a handsome contribution to the viability of the railways of Cornwall and Britain.

In preparing this book I have relied on a number of fellow railway photographers and to all contributors I express my sincere thanks and gratitude. My particular thanks go to Norman Searle and George Hemmett (St. Blazey Supervisors), St. Blazey train crews, Dick Riley and also to the authors of all the books shown in the bibliography. Photographs by the author were taken on either 35mm Nikon equipment or 6 × 7 Pentax camera gear. Films were mostly developed by the author but the majority of prints were processed by Del Mercer of Morden, Surrey. My objective in producing this book is to permanently record thousands of facts, create a pictorial impression and to generate a greater awareness and appreciation of the china clay industry and its very distinctive trains and if I achieve this goal, I will be well satisfied.

John A.M. Vaughan
Goring by Sea, West Sussex
October 1986

DISCOVERY, USE, PRODUCTION AND DISTRIBUTION

China Clay is produced from Kaolinite or decomposed granite. A chemist would recognise the substance as hydrated aluminium silicate, which is a chemically inert material. Kaolin was first discovered by the Chinese in the Kaoling Hills in China as long ago as the 7th century AD, although there is some evidence that a form of china clay was used in the manufacture of some vessels one thousand years BC. In Britain the main china clay deposits are found in parts of Cornwall and in one area of South Devon. In its original state, granite is a hard rock produced by the action of great heat, and it forms the high rocky pointed hills or tors on both Dartmoor and Bodmin Moor. Millions of years ago partial decomposition of the granite masses took place when pressures created by disturbances in the earths interior forced hot acidic gases and fluids through the granite strata. This action changed the crystalline feldspar in the granite to a soft white clay known as kaolin or china clay. These areas of alteration within the granite have a funnel-like shape and extend to considerable depths beneath the surface. For this reason china clay pits cannot be back-filled as this would cover up valuable deposits of china clay. The other constituents of the granite are quartz, mica and tourmaline; these form the waste products of china clay extraction. China clay can be described as a relatively fine, white, inert material with a wide range of properties which can be used for many industrial applications.

Whereas china clay deposits are found where they were formed Ball clays, were transported by water from their original source. Ball clays have been used to make pottery since 5,000 BC but the use of English Ball clays started in the late 16th century when clay pipes were introduced for smoking tobacco. By the 17th and 18th centuries, Ball clay was being used on a large scale for pottery. Some fifty million years ago Britain's climate was tropical and humid, with a high rainfall and a geography and landscape very different from that of today. The land was deeply weathered to produce a mantle which was rich in kaolin. This mantle was eroded by fast flowing rivers which deposited their load of sand, gravel, silt and clay downstream either into low lying areas where the flow was checked or into the sea. In the quieter freshwater flood plains and lagoons, seams of very fine kaolinitic clay were laid down. Although subsequent episodes of earth movement and prolonged periods of erosion occurred, some of these clay seams were preserved. Those of commercial value, the Ball clays, have been worked in the South West of England for over two hundred years, either by open pit or underground mining. There are only three Ball clay producing areas in Britain; the Bovey Basin, between Bovey Tracey and Newton Abbot in South Devon, the Petrockstow Basin in North Devon and around Wareham in Dorset's Isle of Purbeck area. These deposits provide an essential raw material for many ceramic industries both at home and abroad. While this book is primarily concerned with china clay, a couple of photographs of Ball clay train workings are featured.

The first man to find deposits of china clay in Britain was a Quaker apothecary from Plymouth called William Cookworthy. He surveyed Devon and Cornwall until, in 1746, he discovered a small deposit at Tregonning Hill, near Helston. Some two years later he found vast deposits of good quality clay at St. Stephen-in-Brannel, near St. Austell. This was later to develop into the substantial china clay area of Hensbarrow Downs which even today comprise the major workings of English China Clays, covering some 180 square kilometers. In the early days it was the potters who had the greatest use of the mineral and such famous names as Wedgwood, Spode and Minton took out leases on clay pits in order to have ready access to the clay which so improved the colour of their products. The potters did not move their works to Cornwall because in those far off days the South West was too remote from the supplies of coal needed for their kilns. There was no national rail network and the shipment of all minerals was by horse and cart and by merchant vessel. However, by 1840 the potters relinquished their leases, leaving the china clay pits to be worked by Cornish families and businessmen.

In the 18th and 19th centuries, china clay was far from being Cornwall's most important mineral and mining activities extended to tin, lead, copper and arsenic. At many of these mines, tramways were laid for the purpose of transporting ore to crushers or smelters and eventually in 1812 to connect mining areas with sea ports. In the early days ore was carried by pack horses to the ports where it was loaded onto small capacity sailing ships for transportation to the large industrial centres. The horses did not return light as they carried back large quantities of coal to supply the steam pumping engines which were used by most mines. The first two such tramways were the Poldice to Portreath Tramway and the Redruth and Chacewater Railway, which were fully operational in 1819 and 1827 respectively. Both these tramways were laid to approximately 4ft. gauge and they were operated by gravity and by horse. Neither of these lines conveyed china clay, being many miles from the china clay pits around St. Austell but they were the pioneers of a very comprehensive network of Cornish mineral lines which had an impact on the clay industry.

During the late 18th and early 19th century the process of extracting china clay was gradually developing but production by today's standards was essentially small scale. Nowadays extremely powerful and remotely controlled monitors or water hoses are used to direct a jet of water at the pit face with enough force to disintegrate the matrix and wash out the clay in one operation. The water pressure now used is in the region of 300p.s.i. Bulldozers are also used for ripping the clay matrix to optimise clay stream density. Stent or waste rock exposed by the high pressure hoses is removed from the bottom of the pits by fleets of mobile plant so that fresh pit faces are continuously available. Years ago a considerable amount of manual labour was involved in these processes and working conditions could be deplorable. In fact, as recently as 1913, over 5,000 clay workers went on strike in order to secure a pay rise from their basic wage of £1 per week. However, back to production. As the pit is developed, front loading shovels are used to strip the overburden around the edges of the pit and all unwanted debris is taken to tips in large dump trucks. To secure one tonne of china clay four to five tonnes of sand, one tonne of micaceous residue, and a tonne of rock and earth must be removed.

The claystream, composed of water, china clay, sand and micaceous residues, flows along the bottom of the pit to the lowest point, from where it is pumped to the sand separation plant. The course sand is removed at this stage and is taken away by conveyor to the sand tips. The clay, water and micaceous residue is then pumped out of the pit and passed to cyclone separators. Some of the residue, called mica, is removed at this stage after which the slurry passes to a series of dewatering tanks. Further refining removes the remaining sand and mica which are then pumped to the settling lagoons. At this stage while still in slurry form, the clay undergoes a number of complex refining processes. Because the physical and chemical properties of the clay in a natural state vary considerably not only from pit to pit but within one pit, most clays are blended to produce clay of the specification required by the customer. Computers are used to select the right proportions and quality control is checked by regular sampling in testing laboratories near the production units. The clay is piped to storage tanks and then to filter presses which produce a putty like substance at 25 per cent moisture. It is then dried in gas-fired driers which produce a lump or pelletised product, both at 10 per cent moisture. Very fine powdered clay at 1 per cent moisture is produced by a milling process. The processes of yesteryear were far cruder and clay was supplied in small lumps but nowadays clay is supplied to customers in bulk powder form, slurry, bagged in sacks or intermediate bulk containers, pelletized, with various specified moisture contents.

In the early days of china clay production, the output was used almost entirely for the manufacture of porcelain and pottery but now less than 10 per cent of china clay production is used for such purposes. In the early 1980s, a total of 80 per cent of all china clay was used in the manufacture of paper and board both as a filler and as a surface coating. China clay is eminently suitable for filling the interstices of the cellulose fibres which are the main constituent of sheet paper. The amount of filler varies considerably with different types of paper and, for example, good quality magazines may by weight contain up to 30 per cent china clay whereas newsprint, if it contains any clay, has generally under 6 per cent. China clay coating improves the papers printability as well as its appearance and feel. As an extension of the pottery use, china clay is used in the wider ceramics industry. This may include such items as wall tiles, glass, sewer pipes, white cement, glazes and enamels. China clay is also used in paints and polymers

Plate 4: Over the decades china clay workings have completely transformed the topography of Hensbarrow Downs near St. Austell. The scenery is often referred to as surrealistic and bizarre with its deep pits, lakes and flat-topped cones. The prevailing colour of the countryside is white but with grass and vegetation beginning to grow over the older abandoned workings. This view near Carthew shows the scale of operations in just one part of the 180 square kilometre area.

J. Vaughan

as it is capable of expanding the more expensive prime colouring pigments in paints. It is used to improve the properties of all kinds of paint. In rubber production china clay is used as a filler. It can give additional strength and resistance to wear and abrasion. China clay may also be used in plastic and rubber sheathings of electrical cables because it improves insulation properties. Other uses include chemicals, fertilisers, insecticides, pharmaceuticals and medicines, leather and textiles. While such facts may seem removed from china clay trains, it is essential to have a broad understanding of the china clay industry to appreciate the loads carried by china clay trains and the geographical locations of users.

By the year 1800 it was clear to the claypit owners that something would need to be done to improve the transportation of their product. In 1791 the harbour of Charlestown, 1½ miles south east of St. Austell, had been built but loads of clay in bulk or in casks (barrels) had to be hauled to the port in three ton horse drawn wagons over quite deplorable roads and tracks. Pentewan Harbour, some 4 miles south of St. Austell, was also rebuilt with, at least in part, an eye on the expanding clay industry. At this time, some of the clay pits were producing only a few hundred tons each year and the total output for Cornwall was only a few thousand tons but there was every chance that Pentewan could break Charlestown's monopoly on the shipment of china clay. More important was the fact that the owner of Pentewan Harbour was also the owner of several clay pits north west of St. Austell, and he eventually promoted the building of the Pentewan Railway. China clay had been shipped from Pentewan from at least the year 1824 but it was 1829 before the approximately 4ft. gauge Pentewan Railway was opened. The railway was worked by horses until 1873 when it was converted to 2ft. 6in. gauge and worked by steam locomotives. It was to be several decades before there was a main line railway through Cornwall and in fact Cornwall was not rail connected to the rest of England until the opening of the Royal Albert Bridge at Saltash in 1859. Thus the honour of being the first railway to convey china clay fell to the Pentewan.

Unfortunately the railway was beset by problems from the outset. Pentewan Harbour was notorious for silting-up and despite quite elaborate precautions, it was a problem that persisted for the whole of its working life. The restrictions in the harbour meant that only small ships could use it and the approaches were far from straightforward, even for experienced mariners. Furthermore, the railway never reached the works sites of the industry it purported to serve and its terminus was just short of the town of St. Austell. There were grand plans to extend the railway into the heart of china clay country but for financial and other reasons these plans never materialized. China clay traffic peaked in 1891 but by 1904 the railway carried only 2 per cent of the county's china clay shipments. The last load of railborne china clay was transported to Pentewan on 29th January 1918 and the railway closed shortly afterwards. In 1985 some narrow gauge track could still be seen at the abandoned harbour.

By the 1860s, china clay production was still in its infancy but with the failing fortunes of Cornwall's other mining interests, clay transportation assumed greater importance. Charlestown was never rail connected and the owners were not always sympathetic to the transport problems of others. Competition became the name of the game and prominent industrialists were exploring the possibilities of using other and probably more suitable harbours. The harbour at Fowey had been surveyed in 1813 and by 1825 a tramway to Carne Point became a possibility. However, despite the natural harbour and deep water available at Fowey, it was Par Harbour which was selected as a likely outlet for sea going vessels. In 1829 authority was given for the building of Par Harbour to commence. It was to be an entirely artificial harbour, it would be tidal, with a 1,200ft. breakwater enclosing some 35 acres. In 1830 some clay producers with deposits close to St. Austell proposed a short railway from St. Austell to Par which would later be extended to St. Stephen, St. Dennis and Roche through the heart of clay country. These plans coincided with the Pentewan Railway extension plans referred to earlier. Despite the rivalry, none of these plans came to fruition — at least at this time. In 1833 a canal from Ponts Mill to Par Harbour was built to transport various ores and in 1835, from Mollinnis, near Bugle, on the edge of the clay district down to Par Harbour, it was proposed that a tramway be built.

There would be a terminus to the first section at Ponts Mill, where the tramway would connect with the canal to Par. It was not until 1839 that work on the tramway started and the first section was completed in 1840, the same year in which Par Harbour was completed. In 1841 work began on the famous Treffry Viaduct which spanned the deep Luxulyan Valley. The structure was also an aqueduct, it contained 200,000cu. ft. of granite, was 650ft. long, 98ft. high, had 10 arches each with a span of 40ft., took 3 years to complete and cost £7,000. Below this was an incline plane with provision for wagons to be taken up and down the plane simultaneously. The planes were powered by two large waterwheels of about 40ft. diameter. The wagons were horse drawn over the other parts of the tramway. In the face of competition from those with an interest in extending the Pentewan Railway, Treffry publicly announced in 1843 his intention to construct a railway from Newquay to link up with his Par to Molinnis route, then virtually complete, and to have a branch line from St. Dennis Junction as far as Hendra Downs and eventually as far as St. Austell via Treviscoe. By this time many of the traditional mining activities had declined and to some extent china clay was to become the saviour of the area. Treffry was also Chairman of the Cornwall Railway Company and in 1844 plans were in hand to provide a rail link from Saltash to Truro and eventually Penzance.

In 1846 the Newquay to Molinnis line was complete as far as Ruthvoes. Work was started on the Hendra branch taking the line as far as Domellick. The next section to Hendra Prazey was by incline with a steeper incline to the top of Hendra Hill. The Hendra Village to Hendra Down incline was opened in 1852. In 1849, after 5 years of effort, the Newquay to St. Dennis Junction line was completed. Treffry was at this time considering a further line from Ponts Mill to Par Harbour to obviate the need for transhipment to barge. Treffry died in 1850 but his successor saw that the Hendra branch was completed in 1852 (near to the site of the present Parkandillick Works). In 1864 a company called the Newquay and Cornwall Junction Railway Company was formed, with the objective of linking the Cornwall Railways main line sidings at Burngullow with the Hendra terminus of the line from St. Dennis. The mistake was made of starting work from the Burngullow end and in 1867 after two years of effort the line only reached Carpella. By the time they reached Drinnick Mill, in 1869, the company ran out of money.

In 1870 an entrepreneur named Roebuck came from London to Cornwall with spare cash to invest. He leased the

Plate 5: This interesting picture from about the turn of the present century shows a triple-headed, albeit horse-drawn, 'train' of overburden being removed from a Cornish china clay pit. Note the primitive track and wagons with men and also quite young boys employed in the industry.

English China Clays

Plate 6: At several locations china clay was transported from the pits to the railheads in 3 ton horse-drawn wagons. In this very old photograph, lumps of clay are transferred to 8 ton railway wagons by hand while in the background a simple crane is used to lift casks of china clay on to the rail vehicles. The little 8 ton capacity wagons include GWR Nos. 31241 and 31056 and Par Harbour No. 3. Unfortunately the location is not known.

English China Clays

Plate 7: In the early days there were simply scores of small china clay companies, and many owned their own railway wagons. These 10 ton capacity wagons belonged to the North and Rose China Clay and Stone Company of St. Austell. Note that the china clay has been loaded into ¼ ton casks (barrels) for transportation to the docks and on to the customers around the Staffordshire Potteries.

English China Clays

Plate 8: This ancient view at Drinnick Mill shows the labour-intensive loading system with men transferring clay from the dries to the railway wagons in wooden wheelbarrows. The wagons here are owned by the West of England China Stone and Clay Company and the Great Beam Clay Company which were established in 1849. Both companies became part of English China Clays Ltd. in April 1919.

English China Clays

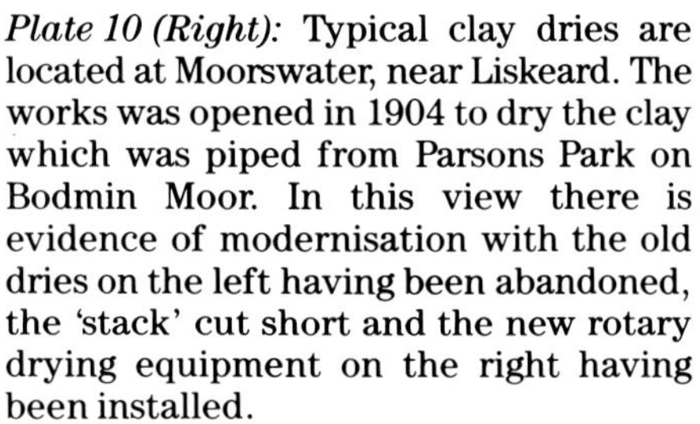

Plate 10 (Right): Typical clay dries are located at Moorswater, near Liskeard. The works was opened in 1904 to dry the clay which was piped from Parsons Park on Bodmin Moor. In this view there is evidence of modernisation with the old dries on the left having been abandoned, the 'stack' cut short and the new rotary drying equipment on the right having been installed.

J. Vaughan

Plate 9: These crude 3-plank wooden wagons were the type of rail vehicle found on the early china clay tramways, many of which were controlled by the Cornwall Minerals Railway. Clay has been loaded into sacks inside the dries. Each of the jute sacks weighed 2cwt. — over 100 kilograms — and loading was not therefore a job to be taken lightly! Note the elderly tank locomotive which, like the location, cannot be identified.

English China Clays

Par to Molinnis and Newquay to Hendra lines from the Trustees of the Treffry Estates with the express intention of linking the two sections. In 1873 he established the Cornwall Minerals Railway (CMR) and plans included steam locomotive operation and a new route up the Luxulyan Valley (which was ready for service in 1874). A most important addition was the proposal to provide a connection with the main line at Par and to build a line from Par to Fowey, which would include a lengthy tunnel at Great Pinnock. In 1874 the CMR was reported as having at Par 18 locomotives costing £2400 each and an "immense" number of trucks. The CMR also built the 'missing' section between Drinnick Mill and Hendra and in 1874 opened branch lines to Carbis and Mellangoose (Retew). The 'main' line from Fowey to Newquay was opened to mineral traffic on 1st June 1874 and to passengers in June 1876. In 1874 Henry Pouchin opened his 2¼ mile Gothers Tramway to Domellick on the St. Dennis to Hendra branch line. The track was laid to 3ft. 1in. gauge. China clay and coal were transported to and from Gothers. In 1877 there was a recession in the china clay industry and with the CMR in financial difficulties the Great Western Railway agreed to work the line. Circumstances improved and in 1893 the CMR built the Goonbarrow and Wheal Rose branches and the GWR took over the Lostwithiel and Fowey Railway, but in 1896 the whole CMR concern was taken over by the GWR, and incorporated in their system.

There had been developments elsewhere with the new 1859 Cornish main line sprouting sidings for the use of china clay trains. A number of clay dries were built, adjacent to the main line, where clay was brought down from the moors and dried before being loaded into rail vehicles. Later still, long distance underground pipelines were installed for this purpose. One notable addition to the china clay train story took place in Devon rather than Cornwall when, in 1854, the Lee Moor Tramway was built to bring down china clay from Lee Moor quarries to Plym Bridge and later Cattewater. The tramway was closed following an accident in 1854 but reopened in 1858. It was laid to the 4ft. 6in. 'Dartmoor Gauge' and included two cable worked inclines to reach its 750ft. summit at Lee Moor. Horses were used on other sections but between the inclines, steam locomotives were used and a photograph of Peckett 0-4-0ST Lee Moor No. 1 of 1899 appears in this book. For most of its life, the line carried substantial loads of china clay down from the hills to the outskirts of Plymouth. In 1921 a large clay drying and processing plant was opened at Marsh Mills, near Tavistock Junction and clay was piped down from the moors. The works still operates and has its own rail connection which runs over a small section of the long abandoned Plymouth to Launceston branch line, where the Plym Valley Railway Company hopes to preserve some of the line. Traffic on the Lee Moor Tramway gradually dwindled, and it fell into disuse in 1939. It was resuscitated during the Second World War but a new 6 mile pipeline from Lee Moor to Marsh Mills was opened in 1947 and finally a slow death resulted in closure in 1960 and rail removal in 1961/2.

In 1911 the Redlake Tramway was opened from Ivybridge up to a clay pit on Dartmoor. The 7½ mile long 3ft. gauge line rose by over 1000ft. to reach the works. The tramway carried only coal, sand and manpower, the clay being piped to a siding on the main line at Ivybridge. The tramway survived for only 21 years being closed in 1932. The trackbed is now a footpath. The now closed BR siding was used for loading china clay until the early 1980s.

The Torrington and Marland Light Railway was another china clay line in Devon. It was built by the Marland and North Devon Clay Company and opened in 1880. The 3ft gauge line was used to transport clay from Marland to Torrington for shipment by barge to Bideford. The 6 mile line was taken over by the North Devon and Cornwall Junction Railway in 1925 and except for the clay works network, converted to standard gauge. Clay continued to be produced at Marland (and Meeth) and was transported by rail to Exeter and beyond but the track gradually deteriorated and without heavy expenditure the heavy new generation wagons could not be supported. The entire line from Barnstaple Junction to Meeth was closed in November 1982.

The Bodmin and Wadebridge Railway was opened in 1834 and it became the first line in Cornwall to use locomotives for haulage. China clay was not one of its payloads until the year 1862 and ironically in the final decades of its life the clay traffic was the only reason for its survival. The line was later taken over by the London and South Western Railway and was worked for many years by the famous 2-4-0 Beattie well tank steam locomotives.

For a number of years china clay was shipped from the quays at Wadebridge and Padstow. But eventually it all travelled via the GWR to Lostwithiel. China clay was transported by pipeline from Stannon on Bodmin Moor to the Stannon clay dries, just short of the Wenford Bridge terminus. The line came into BR ownership and after changes in regional allocation, the ancient line settled down to survive the closure of nearby passenger services from Halwill to Wadebridge, Wadebridge to Padstow, Wadebridge to Bodmin North and General and even Bodmin General to Bodmin Road (now Parkway). However, after services were reduced to 'thrice weekly as and when required' the writing was on the wall and under the new Cornish Railway management the line finally closed completely in 1983.

Plate 11: This view shows the tidal and artificial harbour at Par. The harbour was fully operative in 1840. The port was extensively modernised in 1961 and purchased by English China Clays in 1964. In this view from the 1950s the coaster *Simultineity* is being loaded, while on the right can be seen one of the steam locomotive shunters, with cut-down cab.

R. C. Riley

Plate 12: In this 1910 view of Fowey Docks the application of the end opening wagon can be seen. Mechanisation is already making an impact with the use of the then modern tipping equipment. Behind the two Toyne Carter and Company wagons is an invader from the London and North Western Railway, which is not fitted for end opening.

English China Clays

Plate 14 (Right): There is much to absorb in this superb study of Fowey Station in Edwardian times. Passenger trains from St. Blazey and to Lostwithiel can be seen in the company of a 2-6-2 prairie tank and a remarkable brass-domed saddle tank, possibly one of the 850 class. Most of the china clay seems to be loaded in the large size ½ ton casks in GWR wagons, although there is one interloper from South Wales. After closure to passengers and the lifting of the direct line to Par, this entire site was razed, and in 1968 converted to a road for main access to the docks.

English China Clays

Plate 13: Significant developments took place at Fowey in 1968 when English China Clays leased the docks from British Rail. ECC installed sophisticated rapid loading equipment, slurry tanks and a large clay store. The Clay Hood on the left has just been unloaded and is about to pass on to the automatic traverser for return down the empties road.

J. Vaughan

After temporary closure in 1880, the line from Lostwithiel to Fowey was rebuilt as a standard gauge line by the GWR and reopened in 1895. The line was mainly used by clay from the centres east of Lostwithiel, such as Moorswater, Marsh Mills and Newton Abbot. The line was temporarily closed during both World Wars. Eventually the line was to become the only railway connection to the port of Fowey, after passenger services were withdrawn and the direct line from Par to Fowey was closed (and later converted into a road for the exclusive use of lorries carrying china clay to Fowey Docks). After the Moorswater dries were opened in 1904, clay trains started to use the GWR's 1901 constructed spur from Liskeard to Coombe Junction on the Looe branch but initially some clay was shipped from Looe. The transportation of china clay was revolutionised in the latter part of the 19th century when pipelines were introduced, which meant clay could be carried miles from the pit to the loading point. Despite limited flexibility and a high capital outlay networks blossomed. As a result of this a large number of clay driers appeared on both branches and main line such as Trenance near St. Austell and Hawks Tor, Onslow Sidings near Bodmin Road; a clay dry which received its clay by pipeline from Hawks Tor on Bodmin Moor, some 7 miles away. Most of these dries have since been abandoned. Although the pattern of clay traffic was ever changing and remote sidings were added to or removed from the rail system by the turn of the century, all the main routes had been established, the GWR were in control and there was a period of consolidation. For a few years around the turn of the century, some locally produced china clay was shipped from Penzance Harbour.

There were still to be some additions to the rail network for the purpose of conveying china clay, such as the extension of the Retew branch down to Meledor Mill in 1912 and the opening of the Bojea branch from a point just west of St. Austell to Lansalson in May 1920. However, roads were improving all the time, technology was gradually changing the face of a once labour intensive industry, pipeline technology became more efficient and some areas became worked out or produced clay of an unmarketable quality. Slowly the tide turned as the general depression of the 1920s and 1930s affected the china clay scene. Gothers Tramway near St. Dennis closed in 1933 and the Lee Moor line effectively closed in 1939. In the so-called Beeching era the railway map changed substantially with the Wheal Rose branch at Bugle closing in 1964 and both the Ponts Mill to Trevanney Kiln line and most of the Goonbarrow branch in 1965, St. Dennis Junction to Parkandillick in 1966, the Lansalson branch and Par to Fowey line in 1968, the Retew branch by the early 1980s and Wenford Bridge in 1983. These and most of the surviving branches and installations are illustrated within these pages.

As regards the transportation and distribution of china clay, the story starts with a ponderous horse and cart and ends up with a sophisticated computerised system. A dramatic change took place after the First World War when surplus War Department lorries were readily and cheaply available, and they quickly replaced the horses and carts which had been conveying clay by road and track for over

Plate 15: The holidaymakers who now flock to the resort of Newquay would scarcely recognise this 19th century view of the harbour. While half a dozen 50 ton schooners wait for loading there appears to be only two china clay wagons on the primitive quay. The railway was opened in 1849 and finally closed in 1926 but it had been in decline since 1874 when the line was opened from St. Dennis Junction to the more accessable southern ports of Par and Fowey.

English China Clays

Plate 16: Around the time of World War I, locally produced china clay was exported from Penzance. Most of the clay came from Balleswidden and Leswidden pits near Lands End. This photograph was probably taken in 1919 because the Norwegian ship *SPES* was built in 1918 and mechanical scoop conveyors were supplied in 1920. Here an old steam crane lifts the china clay from vintage steam lorries — one of which has a trailer.

English China Clays

Plate 17: This fascinating view shows the remains of Pentewan Harbour and Railway in April 1985. For years the owners tried to prevent Pentewan from silting-up but especially after the railway closed in 1918 the battle was gradually lost. The sand-filled harbour is on the left while, on the right, (and on the old jetty) can be seen the remains of the 2ft. 6in. gauge track once used by the Pentewan but later by a concrete company who used the dock area until they closed their works in 1966. The last trading vessel called here in 1940.

J. Vaughan

Plate 18: Not only was china clay brought down to St. Austell from many pits by horse, but until 1872 it was then transported from there to Pentewan by horse — on the Pentewan Railway. The team of three horses had just arrived at the St. Austell terminus of the Pentewan with a wagon containing three tons of china clay. Judging by the foreground there must have been plenty of rain in the winter of 1910. West Hill is behind and the site is now occupied by a Co-op supermarket.

English China Clays

Plate 19: In this delightful view, 1901 Manning Wardle-built 0-6-2ST *Canopus* passes the lower reservoir near Pentewan with a single empty wagon. The white washing above the old lime kiln is unlikely to be improved by the emissions from the 11½ ton locomotive's chimney. As stated in the text, the Pentewan never penetrated china clay country — the harbour silted-up and uneconomic working resulted in closure of the railway in 1918.

Locomotive Publishing Company (courtesy Dr. M. J. T. Lewis)

Plate 20: Other than for clay works wagon-ways, the narrow gauge Pentewan Railway was the first in Cornwall to carry china clay. Opened as a horse-operated tramway in 1829, the Pentewan connected the town of St. Austell with the harbour at Pentewan. From 1873 the railway was converted from 4ft. to 2ft. 6in. gauge and worked by steam locomotives. On 14th August 1912, Yorkshire Engine Co.-built 2-6-2ST *Pioneer* nears Pentewan.

The late Albert J. Fellows (courtesy Dr. M. J. T. Lewis)

Plate 21: Although of somewhat dubious quality, this very interesting old photograph shows the manual loading of clay wagons belonging to the North Cornwall China Clay Company Ltd. at Stannon clay dries on the Wenford Bridge line. Clay was carried on the line from 1862 until its demise in 1983. In the early days the clay was off-loaded at Wadebridge and Padstow, but in later years it was conveyed via the GWR to Fowey. The photograph was probably taken early in the present century.

English China Clays

Plate 22: In most china clay and china stone pits there were often complex tramway systems to convey china clay and waste materials from one point to another. Quite often propulsion was by ropeway or cableway and stationary engines. There are plenty of tramways in this view of Nanpean China Stone Quarry, including an inclined narrow gauge line on the right. At the very bottom of the pit can be seen a small wagon turntable. There was a considerable demand for china stone between the wars.

English China Clays

Plate 23: A visit to the Wheal Martyn museum, just north of St. Austell (and Lansalson), is highly recommended, especially for those wanting to secure information about the china clay industry and its history. Two highly appropriate exhibits are steam locomotives with strong china clay connections. This view shows on the left *Lee Moor No. 1,* an 0-4-0 saddle tank built by Peckett in 1899, and right *Judy,* a Bagnall 0-4-0 saddle tank of 1937 with cut-down cab for use in Par Harbour.

J. Vaughan

100 years. This has now developed into the high capacity aluminium bodied tipper trucks which can be seen in action today. The small 50 ton capacity sailing ships have also made way for large ocean-going bulk cargo ships of up to 12,000 tonnes which can be loaded at high speed by modern machinery. As detailed in the relevant sections, there were significant developments at the ports of Par and Fowey to accommodate the high throughput of china clay for shipment — for example approximately 1.4 million tonnes of clay were handled at Fowey in the year 1985. Long distance pipelines were constructed forming a complete underground network between the pits and the clay dries or ports. All china clay train movements have always been controlled in Cornwall from the offices at St. Blazey and over the years a paper driven system has given over to firstly Telex and more recently, computer systems. It is only too easy to underestimate the difficulty in ensuring that with a few hours notice, clay of a certain quality can be collected from a clay works and delivered to a port with the minimum of fuss, or that a particular rake of wagons is in exactly the right place at the right time.

In the early days the lumps of clay were carried in crude open wooden framed and bodied goods wagons, and jute sacks and wooden barrels (or 'casks') were simply loaded one upon another. It often rains in Cornwall and loads can easily be contaminated by moisture or other substances. While it is easy to handle china clay slurry, it is a very different story when it comes to loading but particularly unloading china clay which contains more moisture than the receiving system was designed to handle. A form of sheeting was perfected using at first tarpaulins but later modern rubberised materials. The early wagons were of 3, 5 and 7 side plank construction. They were without brakes and indeed, because of the cloying slime in the pits and at the docks, vacuum brake fittings were ruled out. For well over a century the little 4-wheeled clay wagons stopped to have their brakes pinned down by hand before negotiating severe gradients. However, in a major uplift in about 1970, vacuum brakes were fitted and for local trip workings the payload of rail wagons increased from about 10 to 12.5 tons! In 1895 the GWR stipulated the dimensions and loading system for china clay wagons and in fact most of the present wooden bodied 4-wheelers built at Swindon from about 1955 were built broadly to these GWR dimensions, retaining the facility of side doors for casks. In 1914 the clay wagon fleet had grown to 800 wagons which were owned by the GWR, clay producers, shipping agents and port authorities. After the Second World War, the Ministry of Transport took over the 4-wheeled 'Clay-tip' fleet before handing over to British Railways on Nationalization in 1948. The conventional covering system for the clay wagons comprised a separate BR sheet which was secured by a number of ties to jambing cleats on the wagon. The arrangement was unsatisfactory. Sheets had to be removed for loading and unloading, became dirty and torn, held water in the corners and developed pinholes which allowed water to contaminate the clay. The heaped load shifted during transportation which altered tensioning. When ties became knotted staff often cut them to release and the system was generally inconvenient.

The wagon fleet reached a peak of nearly 900 wagons but by about 1970 when the port of Fowey was being further developed a new covering system was discussed, evaluated, agreed and eventually jointly financed by BR and ECC. All parties realised that the wagon fleet was already out of date but nobody was anxious to invest vast sums on new builds. The fleet was rationalised to 674 wagons and several experiments were conducted with covers. These included examining fibreglass canopies (only used on road vehicles), fitting 'pram hood' covers, triple bar and single ridge bar designs. Various treatments to the wooden sided wagons were also tried. Eventually, after a number of teething troubles were overcome, the 'Clay Hood' was perfected. From 1974 BR Horwich Works produced conversion kits which were assembled at the BR Wagon Works at St. Blazey. Although old style wagons were used to serve customers as far away as Fort William in Scotland (until the introduction of high capacity air-braked vehicles from 1982) the Clay Hoods were restricted to use in Devon and Cornwall. By 1985 only 500 Clay Hoods remained in use. All of the Clay Hood fleet is restricted to 45 mph.

The variety of railway wagon currently carrying some form of china clay is almost infinite. From the late 1960s, clay was transported by rail in slurry form in 2 axle 32 tonne tank wagons which worked to Sittingbourne in Kent and later to Scotland. Other larger bogie tankers now work to Warrington in Lancashire. There are the 80 tonne gross weight Polybulk wagons which cater for international traffic to Switzerland and the lengthy VTG and Ferrywagons which also cross the English Channel with heavy payloads of packaged clay. Covered wagons from the European Danzas and Cargowagon firms also visit Cornwall regularly to collect bagged and palletted clay and Transfesa fruit wagons can also call for a back load to Spain. From Scotland come the Tullis Russell wagons, designed and leased by Tiger — built by Procor, and PRA air-braked vehicles which serve the West Highlands. BR's Railfreight service uses various covered wagons including the VAB, VDA and VGA types but the old fashioned box van now seems to have disappeared from the china clay scene. Then there is the new French built Tiger 55 type of wagon for delivery to customers within the UK which seem to spend most of their time running from Cornwall to Cliffe Vale, Stoke-on-Trent and Mossend Yard, Glasgow. All of these wagons have a unique function for a particular load. All but the Railfreight wagons are either owned or leased by customer companies, although the Tiger wagons bear the insignia ECC International. Most wagons visit most pits but not all wagons visit all pits. The permutation of movement is determined by supply and demand, but the subject is fascinating and provides plenty of variety for the observer and photographer of china clay trains. Rail operations are truly international and the conveyance of china clay is a very sizeable contributor to the viability of railways in Cornwall. Many of the wagons referred to are illustrated within these pages.

During 1985/6 it became clear to all concerned that the 30 year old Clay Hoods with their wooden bodies and vacuum brakes were life expired. It was considered that local china clay trip workings in the south west should be taken over by large capacity, air braked, roller bearing rail wagons which would, if necessary, be compatible with the long distance air braked vehicles. As a result of the 1984/5 coal miners strike road vehicles made inroads into the well established "merry-go-round" coal field to power station services and consequently a number of HAA hopper wagons of the required specification became available. Despite the initial absence of a suitable wagon covering system trials were conducted in the early part of 1986 with two specially cleaned wagons. The 17 tonne wagons had a tare capacity of 33 tonnes and an all up weight of about 50 tonnes. It was expected that by the end of 1987 most of the Clay Hoods would be withdrawn. In January 1987 tenders were issued for 124 new purpose built air-braked CDA wagons.

ST. BLAZEY

St. Blazey takes its name from Bishop Blaize, the patron saint of woolcombers. The railway depot started life in the 1850s when a tramway was constructed from Ponts Mill to Par Harbour. Under the auspices of the Cornwall Mineral Railway, a branch from St. Blazey to Fowey was opened in 1873 and the 1855 tramway to Molinnis was opened up to Newquay in 1874. A through passenger service from Fowey to Newquay started in 1876 and a station carrying the name Par was opened at St. Blazey. Many buildings were erected on the St. Blazey site and the unusual engine shed and adjacent buildings which survive to this day were once the works of the CMR. The Cornwall Railway's main line from Saltash to Penzance crossed the CMR just south of St. Blazey and a single track connection between the main line and the CMR was built. This was doubled in 1870 and when the main line Par station opened, the earlier CMR station became St. Blazey. The St. Blazey to Fowey line closed to passengers in 1929, although it was used by workmens' trains for another 5 years. The station buildings were finally demolished in the 1970s.

For nearly a century, St. Blazey has been an important centre for china clay train marshalling and control. Indeed in 1986 the BR movements Supervisor still resides at St. Blazey. Above all else St. Blazey has been the motive power nerve centre for the clay lines. Back in 1873 the CMR had 18 steam locomotives built by Sharp Stewart and they were designed to work 'back to back' (i.e. bunker to bunker) and this may account for the nine-road round house. Some of these locomotives were absorbed by the GWR in 1895 and the last was not withdrawn until 1936 with the running number 1400. St. Blazey had an allocation of 35 steam locomotives for clay and other freight duties. These were nearly all tank locomotives. In the early days Wolverhampton built 0-6-0 pannier tanks of the 2021 and 2181 class worked the clay lines. In later years they were replaced by 4500 class 2-6-2 prairie tanks and the 1600(5700) class 0-6-0 pannier tanks. To work the steeply graded line from Par to Fowey two Class 4200 2-8-0 or 7200 2-8-2 tanks were employed. They could take nearly twice the load of a 2-6-2T. Generally the small pannier tanks had the best route availability and were used on the lines with small radius curves. Tender locomotives were used on the main line turns and on some of the few passenger services in the area worked by St. Blazey men.

The first main line diesel locomotives arrived in 1958 but it was 1960 before they impinged on the china clay scene to any extent. The original Class 41 'Warships' and the more numerous Class 42 and 43 B-B 'Warships' of 2,000h.p. and 2,200h.p. respectively were followed by the small 1,000h.p. North British Class 22. The high availability of the diesels meant that one diesel could sometimes replace three steam locomotives. By 1964 the steam locomotive had been completely replaced and the only whiff of steam was from the Par Harbour shunters. The 'Clayliner' service developed and this resulted in the regular appearance of type 4 diesel locomotives on china clay trains travelling to Severn Tunnel Junction and then to the Potteries at Stoke-on-Trent and even Scotland. The 2,700h.p. Class 52 'Westerns' made regular appearances and they were closely followed in the mid 1960s by the ubiquitous Class 47s. BR announced that the diesel hydraulic fleet, which was all but unique to the Western Region, would be phased out and this gradually brought the heavy Class 45 and 46 'Peaks' into the area. By 1971 the Class 22s had been scrapped and Class 25s with 1,250h.p. Sulzer engines were transferred from the London Midland Region. In the mid 1970s, 2,700h.p. 100 m.p.h. Class 50s started to replace the 'Westerns' and on occasions they also found themselves hauling china clay trains. The last diesel hydraulic was withdrawn in 1977 and the relatively short term stay of the Class 25s came to an end in 1980, when they were transferred in favour of 1,750h.p. Class 37s which were moved to Cornwall from South Wales. The first two Class 37s arrived in 1978 and at the time of writing, up to 4 locomotives of the class work all china clay trains excepts those ABS services which run to and from Severn Tunnel Junction and local trips handled by Class 08 shunters. The Class 37s are allocated to Plymouth Laira but are normally shedded at St. Blazey, as are the regular type 4 visitors. One Class 37 was named *William Cookworthy* to

Plate 24 (left): Part of St. Blazey locomotive depot still operates on the 'roundhouse and turntable' principle, nowadays an anachronism and a left-over from the days of steam. Proudly showing the Cornish Railways insignia, No. 37207 *William Cookworthy* (named after the UK discoverer of china clay) positively gleams from the decaying buildings on 17th May 1984. Between 1983 and 1986, Cornwall was given delegated responsibility for running and financing its railways.

J. Vaughan

Plate 25 (Right): With the now demolished St. Blazey (formerly Par) Station visible above the GWR 'toad' brake van, the 08.10 clay empties to Goonbarrow leaves St. Blazey Yard. Photographed on 8th July 1955, the locomotive was one of the then modern Hawksworth 0-6-0 pannier tanks of 1949 build — 1600 class No. 1626. The engine shed and wagon works can be seen in the left background.

R. C. Riley

celebrate the association of the locomotive type with the china clay industry and another by the Cornish name *Tre Pol and Pen.* On the shunter front, Class 08s have been a feature for many years and only Class 03s and Class 10s have ever challenged their rule. In 1986 St. Blazey's permanent allocation had shrunk to just two Class 08 shunters. Happily many of the old buildings at St. Blazey survive, albeit in run down condition, the depot turntable is still operational, there is a wagon works (see captions) and manual semaphore signalling is extant. This situation is unlikely to continue for much longer.

Plate 26: In the age of plastics, alloys and the microchip, a remarkable survivor from the days when wood and iron were supreme is St. Blazey Wagon Works. The works is charged with the task of maintaining and repairing wooden-sided wagons which in many cases are already thirty years old. In this March 1984 view, the new planks in the sides and end of OOV No. 743153 can be seen. These wagons no longer make long-distance journeys but they are used locally, and so for the time being the craftsmen of St. Blazey can continue to practise their trade.

J. Vaughan

Plate 27: The exterior of St. Blazey Wagon Works with nineteen wheel/axle units in the foreground. During 1974/5, the works converted most of the UCV/OOV wagons to Clay Hoods, using special kits manufactured at BREL Horwich. The works manages to keep several hundred of the old wooden-sided wagons running and they also maintain and repair much of the modern large capacity air-braked fleet.

J. Vaughan

Plate 28: Once the diesels arrived at St. Blazey, the demise of the steam locomotive was rapid. The high availability rate of the diesels meant that a single diesel could replace three steam locomotives, reducing St. Blazey's allocation from about 35 to 12. In the early days of dieselisation the Class 41/42/43 'Warships' were followed by the small Class 22s and the large Class 52 'Westerns' on china clay workings, but all are now extinct on BR. On 20th July 1960, No. D816 *Eclipse* prepares to leave St. Blazey for Fowey.

R. C. Riley

Plate 29: Nowadays, St. Blazey's locomotive allocation extends to just two Class 08 shunters. However, although notionally allocated to Plymouth (Laira), most of the china clay traffic is handled by four Class 37s (and one or two visiting 'Type 4s'), which are the normal residents of St. Blazey depot. On 2nd March 1984, No. 47283 is revolved on St. Blazey's turntable.

J. Vaughan

PAR HARBOUR

Plate 30: In front of the vast clay works at Par Harbour, sporting the words English China Clays Group, is the famous *Alfred.* Bagnall's allocated the number 3058 to *Alfred* in 1953 when the locomotive was built, specifically for use in the Par Harbour complex. On the right is a Wolverton-built 45m.p.h. restricted box van, No. 760290, which contains bagged china clay.

English China Clays

Plate 31: Par Harbour had its share of sentinel/internal combustion-engined shunters to move clay wagons around its once extensive rail system. By the mid-1950s, the remains of a 1927-built sentinel, called *Toby,* were rusting away behind the diminutive docks shed, but this photograph shows a later arrival. Note the chain drive and sanding gear. Specially adapted road-going tractors were also used for shunting in the port.

C. H. A. Townley

Plate 32: Nowadays, most of the harbour railway complex has been closed and the only rail traffic is an 'as required' trip working from St. Blazey Yard. After the branch line from St. Blazey to Fowey was closed in 1968 and converted to a private road for the exclusive use of ECC lorries, road transport has made greater use of Par Harbour. Most of the clay arrives by pipeline and it is only the products of the bagging plant which leave Par Harbour by rail. About 1,800 ships per annum use Par Harbour and over one million tonnes of china clay is exported each year. On 16th May 1984, No. 08945 leaves the harbour and makes for St. Blazey with two wagons.

J. Vaughan

Plate 33: (Right): With the rusting and weed-covered tracks on the right acting as testimony to the once extensive Par Harbour railway network, No. 08113 stops at the extremity of current BR working and deposits three wagons, on 16th June 1982. Notice the steam coming from the tall chimneys of the drying plant.

J. Vaughan

Par Harbour is completely artificial having been constructed in the 1830s to compete with the harbour at Charlestown and to a lesser extent, Pentewan. The harbour at Par was completed in 1840 to receive china clay (and many other minerals) by barge from Ponts Mill (and other mines or consoles) for transfer to sailing ships. The harbour served mainly the copper and tin mines yet slowly but surely china clay began to make an impression and eventually became the only reason for the port's existence. An earlier harbour once existed inland and indeed centuries ago high tides used to reach the Ponts Mill area until this silted up with spoil from the mines.

Over the years the size of ships increased but being tidal, Par can only accommodate small coasters. Popular destinations have been Ridham Dock in North Kent, the Thames, the Manchester Ship Canal, Scotland and the Beneluxe ports. In 1946 English China Clays took over the port on a 999 year lease and in 1964 they bought it outright. In 1961 the port was modernised and enlarged and there are now 10 berths of up to 280ft/85 metres in length. All the quays are now concrete and modern vessels of up to 2,000 tonnes dead weight can be accommodated. The port is still tidal and dries out at low water but this is an impressive growth for a port originally conceived in the days of the 50ft. Schooner.

Most of the china clay is piped to Par Harbour from works up to 11 miles away. There it is dried and steam can be seen coming from the tall chimneys 24 hours per day. Much of the processed clay is taken by the private road, built in 1968 on the trackbed of the old Par to Fowey railway line, to Fowey in large 4 axle lorries, which are purpose built and owned by ECC. This novel application takes much road traffic off Cornwall's narrow roads. The works at Par Harbour is also a mill and bagging plant and nowadays the only regular railborne traffic is bagged clay in covered rail wagons. A Class 08 shunter works down to the harbour once or twice a day, as required and as illustrated. There were two points of rail access but the one from the west, which left the main line at Par Harbour signalbox (now demolished), was abandoned in the 1960s.

Par Harbour was well known for its own industrial engines. All locomotives had cut down cabs to work under low bridges. Before the Second World War steam locomotives called *Punch* and *Judy* were used with a 1927 built sentinel called *Toby*, but later two Bagnall 0-4-0 saddle tanks were used, including *Judy* and the well known *Alfred*. These two locomotives have been preserved; *Judy* on static exhibit at Wheal Martyn Museum, north of St. Austell but *Alfred* by the Cornish Steam Locomotives group at Bodmin General Station.

RAIL ROUTES TO FOWEY

Plate 34 (Below): The branch from Lostwithiel to Carne Point, Fowey, is very picturesque running along the banks of the River Fowey estuary for its entire five mile length. During 1985, Class 37 No. 37196 was painted in BR's new Railfreight livery and it received the very Cornish name of *Tre Pol and Pen.* On 19th August 1985, *Tre Pol and Pen* was 'mated' with *William Cookworthy* on a Goonbarrow to Carne Point working, and the Cornish pair were photographed leaving the main line at Lostwithiel to start their journey to Fowey.

J. Vaughan

Plate 35 (Right): One of the most delightful and tranquil places in the whole of Cornwall to sit and watch china clay trains is the tiny churchyard at St. Winnow, near Lostwithiel. Although there can be a gap of several hours between trains on some days, at other times there is plenty of action as a procession of clay trains rumble down the branch to feed the hungry vessels waiting at Fowey Docks. Looking across the River Fowey, No. 37.207 *William Cookworthy* leads No. 37.181 towards Carne Point on 22nd August 1985.

J. Vaughan

Plate 36 (Below Right): The only intermediate road access to the Fowey branch is at the small harbour of Golant, which was served by a railway halt until passenger services were withdrawn in 1965. The views of the railway in, around, and above the hamlet are magnificent. With the shadows lengthening towards the end of a perfect day, Nos. 37.222 and 37.196 *Tre Pol and Pen* driven by Don Tregaskes pass Golant on 3rd October 1985 with a long string of empty clay hoods returning to Lostwithiel.

J. Vaughan

Plate 37: Once the BR locomotives have delivered their load to the sidings at Carne Point they must be shunted towards the unloader. The choice of motive power for this activity was rather unusual in the shape of two Class 10 370hp Blackstone-engined shunters, which were made redundant by BR many years ago. No. D3497 is now derelict on the quayside where it is a source of spare parts, as seen here on the right, while No. D3476 and its match wagon pass with a long rake of china clay wagons. Carne Point signal box was closed in 1954. A class 08 replaced the Class 10s in 1986.

J. Vaughan

Plate 38: This old disused wagon turntable was photographed at Fowey on 11th June 1981. It was probably last used before the modern automatic traverser was installed. Such relics are forever dwindling on the railway scene as modernisation sweeps all else aside.

J. Vaughan

Plate 39 (Below): From 1895 the GWR took over both of the railway lines to the town of Fowey and they set about improving the docks area. Eventually they owned 800yds. of jetty frontage, provided facilities for the rapid loading of clay on to large sea-going vessels, and set up a suitable transport infrastructure commensurate with a rapidly developing clay industry. The most significant developments took place from 1968 when English China Clays leased the deep water jetties from BR and instigated a major development project. On 21st November 1983, No. D3476 propels some Clay Hoods towards the unloader.

J. Vaughan

Plate 40 (Right): A picture which well illustrates the transition from steam to diesel. On 22nd July 1960, Collett 0-4-2T No. 1419 pauses at the southern end of Fowey Station between passenger workings to Lostwithiel while on the left a train of clay empties is about to depart along the now closed line to Par behind green-liveried Class 42 'Warship' *Eclipse*. These diesels had remarkable versatility hauling a long clay train at 20m.p.h. on a Cornish branch line one day and leaving Paddington with a 90m.p.h. express the next.

R. C. Riley

The harbour at Fowey has a history going back many hundreds of years. However, it was in the late 18th and early 19th century that its many attributes came to the attention of the mine owners. Fowey is a natural deep water port but it is strange to relate that freight transportation to the docks was by horse and cart until the 1869 to 1873 period, when the town was approached from two directions by the railway builders.

In 1869 the Lostwithiel and Fowey Railway had opened a broad gauge freight only line to Carne Point, just short of Fowey. The line carried mainly clay but at such competitive rates that when heavy engineering works became necessary, it was forced to close through lack of capital and between 1880 and 1895 it was abandoned. The GWR rebuilt the line as a standard gauge route in 1895, linked it to the former Cornwall Minerals Railway route and ran a passenger service to Fowey, which survived until 1965. Ironically this is now the only line to survive and yet the route, for the majority of clay trains, is longer than the closed CMR line, necessitating a reversal of Lostwithiel.

The CMR reached Fowey in 1873 after building a difficult route from Par, which included gradients of 1 in 36 and the 1173yd. Pinnock Tunnel. After the clay business slumped in 1877 the GWR took over the line. A passenger service ran between the years 1876 and 1929, and for workmen until 1934. The line had intermediate sidings and considerable volumes of clay were taken to Fowey. However, following an agreement in the mid-1960s between BR and English China Clays, who had forseen the need for road access to Fowey Docks, which included the use of rail (via Lostwithiel), the line was closed and converted for road use (controlled by traffic lights through the single line tunnel).

The GWR developed Fowey and they once owned 800 yards of jetty frontage for the shipment of clay. Mechanical devices were installed to facilitate high speed loading and, except for the war years and the depression, business boomed. The most significant development was in 1968 when ECC leased the deep water loading jetties from BR. A major development project ensued and the specification now reads, four operational jetties — three equipped for road and rail traffic — one for slurry clay only, a bulk store capable of holding 22,000 tonnes of dry clay and five slurry storage tanks, loaders capable of loading clay onto ships at between 500 and 1,000 tonnes per hour, ability to accept ships up to 12,000 tonnes dead weight and to ship nearly 1½ million tonnes of clay per year (over one third of which arrives in little 12.5 tonne capacity Clay Hoods).

The surviving line from Lostwithiel to Carne Point is extremely picturesque as it runs on mainly level ground along the banks of the Fowey estuary. The branch leaves the main line just south west of Loswithiel station and the only intermediate point of any importance along the single track route is Golant, where there is a small harbour and where there was once a tiny halt. China clay trains traverse the branch from about 05.00 to 18.00 hours Mondays to Fridays, weather, traffic and holiday permitting. There is a minimum of four round trips per day and there can be up to twice this number when ships are waiting or the store needs boosting. There are four main sidings at Fowey and shunting was performed by an ex BR Blackstone-engined Class 10 diesel shunter but a Class 08 was purchased by ECC from BR in 1986. Two wagon traversers are provided in the unloading equipment and an ancient wagon turntable can still be seen, although disused. Modifications for hopper discharge were made over the 1986/7 period. Unauthorised persons are not permitted into the docks however, but the line is a popular venue for special excursions for railway enthusiasts.

Plate 41: One of the modern traction disasters was the North British Class 22 diesels. This example, No. D6342, was introduced in 1962, withdrawn in 1968 and cut-up during 1969. Many of the class worked quite hard in Cornwall and here the little 1,100hp diesel takes a breather as it leaves Pinnock Tunnel on the St. Blazey to Fowey line on 9th May 1963. This line, including the tunnel was converted to a road and is now used exclusively by ECC clay lorries.

C. Batchelor

Plate 42: Normally St. Blazey Depot had two large 2-8-0 tank locomotives for use on the direct line to Fowey. The Class 4200 (or 7200 2-8-2T) could handle twenty loaded clay wagons between St. Blazey and Fowey, whereas, for example, a 2-6-2 prairie was restricted to twelve. On 9th July 1955, No. 4247 trundles down past Par Sands with empties. The line was closed and lifted in 1968.

R. C. Riley

Plate 43: The line seen here is now used only by the daily or so trip working from St. Blazey to Par Harbour. In the days when yellow front ends on diesel locomotives were unknown on BR, a fairly new Class 22 diesel, No. D6325, arrives at St. Blazey with a mixed clay train. The box vans were used for bagged or palleted clay. The Cornish main line can be seen above the train, but alas all of the signals visible in the right background have long disappeared.

R. C. Riley

Plate 44: With the weeds gradually taking over on the siding down to Par Harbour No. 08113 returns to St. Blazey 'light engine' after dropping off some wagons for loading on 16th June 1982. There was once a signal box on the right to control the many rail movements which formerly occurred to both the harbour at Par and the docks at Fowey.

J. Vaughan

PONTS MILL

Plate 45 (Left): Ponts Mill is a wonderful place for a browse (with permission). This once important centre is situated at the foot of the old Carmears Incline (in the Luxulyan Valley), was the transhipment point for clay and minerals from tramway to barge, and the scene of frantic mining activity in the first half of the 19th century. Now the only action is at the little clay-drying plant. Class 08 No. 08945 dwarfs the 'big A' lorry — Gardner-engined Atkinson of 1969 — which is hiding behind some bagged clay.

J. Vaughan

Plate 46 (Below Left): Ponts Mill is located about a mile along the Newquay branch which climbs above the works on its way to Luxulyan. As and when required, but not normally more than once per day, a Class 08 shunter propels a train down to Ponts Mill from St. Blazey as there are no run-round facilities at the works. The train usually works with an air-piped brake van. On 17th May 1984, No. 08945 crosses a river while shunting a handful of wagons.

J. Vaughan

Plate 47 (Above): On 16th April 1985, it was again No. 08945 which worked the Ponts Mill clay train. Here the shunter leaves the Newquay branch and propels its six PRA wagons (the only grab discharge wagons carrying china clay on the air-braked services) and SR Lancing-built brake van to the Ponts Mill clay works. On the left, the single track Newquay branch starts its climb through the Luxulyan Valley. Within 36 hours these wagons will be discharging their load near Fort William in the West Highlands of Scotland.

J. Vaughan

Plate 48 (Below): A general view of a superb location. Before departing with its little freight, No. 08945 earns some rest while the shunter climbs up on the wagons to make sure the elastic cleats are securely fastened on the wagon covers for the long journey ahead. The whole area is seething with the atmosphere of defunct mining activities and, for the explorer, there are rewards to be found — at least in terms of industrial archaeology. May the little works prosper.

J. Vaughan

STEAM IN 1960

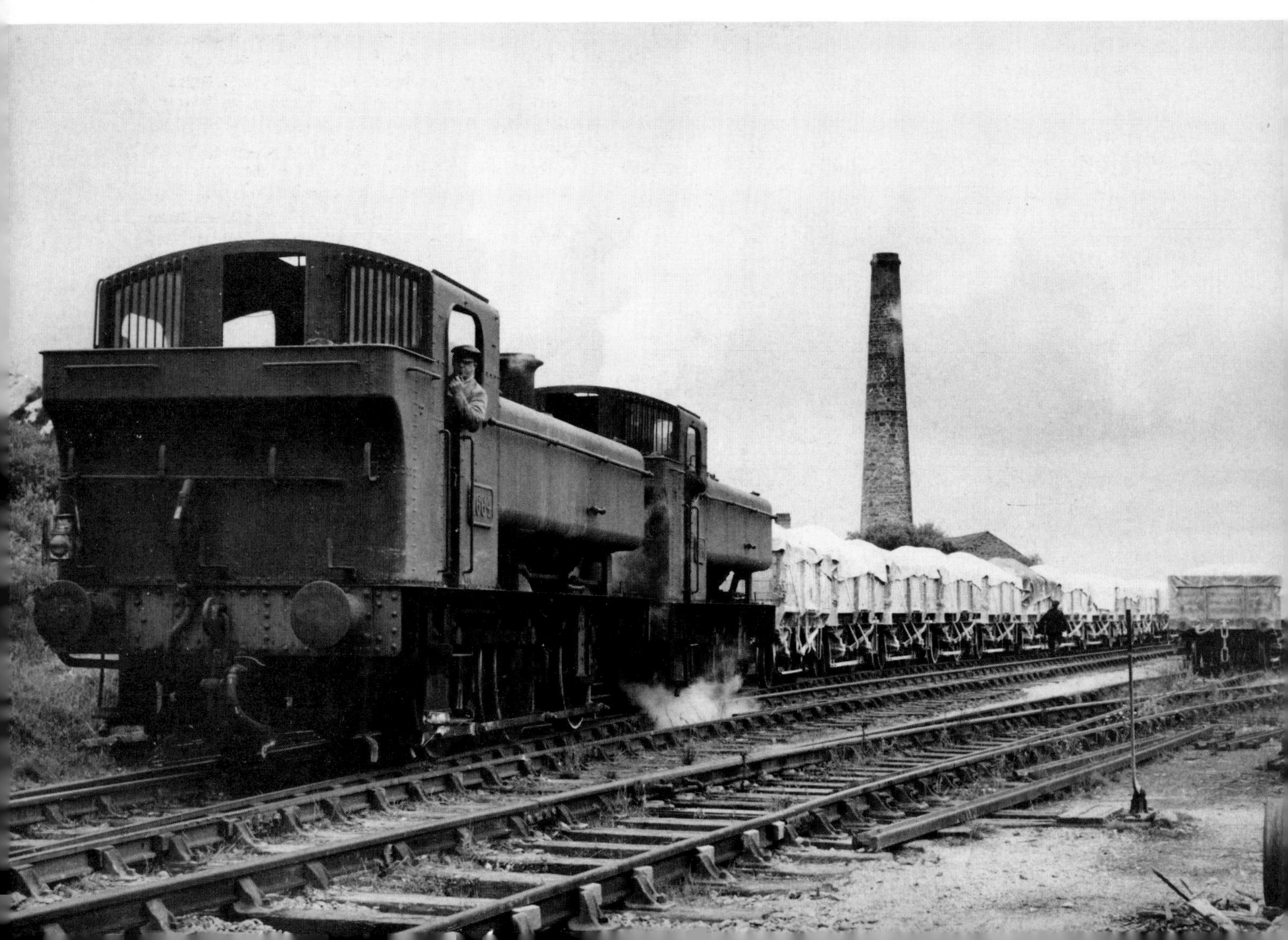

Plate 49 (Left): By 1960 the long reign of the steam locomotive was steadily in decline and the new generation of diesels was starting to make inroads into the number of locomotives required for use on china clay workings. Here, on 25th July, 1960, old stager No. 8737, built in 1929 to a Collett design, arrives at St. Dennis Junction from the Burngullow direction. On the extreme right is the Retew branch.

M. Pope

Plate 50 (Below Left): Having picked up china clay wagons at the many dries along the way, 0-6-0PTs Nos. 1664 and 1626, of the 1949-built 41 ton '1600' class, prepare to leave Goonbarrow Junction with a train from Carbean. The pipe-smoking driver contemplates his next move as the shunter walks to the back of the train.

M. Pope

Plate 51 (Above): The Goonbarrow branch was opened in 1893, but by the time this picture was taken in 1960 the line had only five years to live. In the heart of china clay country at Stenalees, with a Cornish cottage on the left and clay waste pyramids in the distance, a pair of Hawksworth-designed pannier tanks take on water before continuing from Carbean down the steeply-graded branch to Goonbarrow.

M. Pope

Plate 52 (Below): On 26th July 1960, heavy metal was employed on this long rake of clay empties travelling from Fowey to Meledor Mill on the Retew branch. One of the chunky 81 ton 2-8-0T locomotives, designed by Churchward and introduced from 1910, double-heads a 57 ton 2-6-2T Prairie — introduced from 1906 — past Goonbarrow signal box on the Newquay branch. No. 4273 has assisted No. 4559 up the 1 in 37 incline to Luxulyan and will continue to St. Dennis Junction where just the Prairie will take the load down to Mellangoose and Meledor, after running round its train.

M. Pope

GOONBARROW AND RETEW CLAY

Although not the earliest, certainly the most important railway system in the clay district was that of the Cornwall Minerals Railway Company (CMR). The line developed from two horse worked lines built by Joseph Thomas Treffry of Place, Fowey. He was a major mine and landowner and he built standard gauge tramways to transport copper, ore and granite from mines and quarries in the Luxulyan area and clay from the Bugle area to the harbour of Par on the south coast, and Newquay on the north coast. In about 1841 a short line from Colcerrow Quarry to the site of the Treffry Viaduct and Aqueduct was in use but it was the completion of the impressive structure which spanned the Luxulyan Valley which enabled the tramway to make real progress. The viaduct/aqueduct carried the tramway and the leat which provided the water to power the large water wheels that hauled the tramway wagons up the 1 in 10 incline from Ponts Mill. At Ponts Mill minerals were transferred to barges for the short journey by the 1833 built canal to Par Harbour, which had been completed in 1840. The viaduct was completed in 1843 but the tramway incline was not opened until 1847. The inconvenience of transhipment at Ponts Mill resulted in the tramway being extended to Par in 1855, and the closure of the canal shortly afterwards.

The Newquay tramway also began with an incline which at 1 in 4½ ran up from Newquay Harbour through a tunnel to what is now the town, to the site of the present railway station. Wagons were hauled up the incline by cable. It continued over the Trenance Valley on a flimsy timber viaduct and along the alignment of the present Par to Newquay BR line as far as St. Dennis. The only deviation was a short tunnel near Indian Queens which was later avoided when the track was re-aligned. From. St. Dennis the tramway followed the line of the later Newquay and Cornwall Junction line to a terminus at Hendra, via another incline. Short sections were opened from 1846 and in 1852 to Hendra Prazey and Hendra Hill, as mentioned in a previous chapter. These tramways were both early china clay lines delivering the products of the pits to Par and Newquay Harbours. Shipments from Newquay ceased in 1926 when the harbour line closed.

The Cornwall Mineral Railway had an important effect on clay transportation but ironically, after it ceased to exist under its own name; the Great Western Railway having agreed to work the lines from 1877 and later, in 1896, having purchased the entire CMR system. During its short life the CMR achieved a great deal in terms of construction, if not economic viability. Roebuck, the proprietor, had connected the Par and Newquay tramways by 1874, had realigned the route up the Luxulyan Valley and completed a direct route from Par to Fowey. The CMR built branches to Carbis Wharf and (the Retew branch) to Melangoose, closed the gap between Drinnick Mill and the Hendra terminus and provided numerous intermediate sidings. Finally in 1893, when china clay fortunes improved, the Goonbarrow branch was constructed which penetrated deep into the clay country at New Caudletown, and a short branch from Bugle to Wheal Rose was opened.

From St. Blazey Yard the line to Goonbarrow and St.

Plate 53 (Below Left): The line from Par and St. Blazey to Newquay has a long and interesting history which is outlined in the general text. Just before the advent of the 'Tiger' 80 tonne wagons in 1982, No. 50012 *Benbow* brings the wagons for what was once called the 'Clayliner' train into St. Blazey Yard. The provision of three brake vans seems a little excessive because the train will work up without a van, relying for stopping power on the vacuum brakes on the wagons and of course the locomotive. Class 50s are well worth recording on such trains.

J. Vaughan

Plate 54 (Right): On 23rd February 1982, No. 37274 brings eighteen loaded Clay Hoods through the rock-strewn Luxulyan Valley from the Goonbarrow direction. The photograph was taken from the then 140 year old Treffry Viaduct/Aquaduct, once crossed by a mineral tramway, which was superseded by the line shown here in 1874. Traditional deciduous trees have not given way to the ubiquitous conifers, so loved by the Forestry Commission, and hence the valley still reflects the 'seasons' of the year.

J. Vaughan

Plate 55 (Below): In days of old when the environment was not subjected to the interest of pressure groups and some industrialists were not particularly responsible, all the rivers in china clay areas were white with the discharges from clay workings and at some earlier tin works where clay was present as a nuisance. In the late 1960s and early 1970s, the English China Clays Group went to enormous trouble and expense to eliminate all such discharges and nowadays the rivers run clear, as seen here. Having climbed almost 400ft. from St. Blazey, No. 37185 curves through Luxulyan with the 13.55 clay empties to Goonbarrow Junction, on 28th February 1984. Note the light bullhead rail and the 30m.p.h. speed restriction — investment is well overdue!

J. Vaughan

Plate 56 (Above Left): This April 1983 scene at ECC Rocks Works, Goonbarrow Junction shows, on the right, the Newquay branch and some 'Turbot' wagons, right centre, No. 37272 and a single PRA clay wagon, and left centre, the line on the route which once formed the Goonbarrow branch to Stanalees and Gunheath. On the left, ECC 0-4-0 Rolls Royce-powered Sentinel shunter makes progress over the sidings to the clay works.

J. Vaughan

New Plate 57 (Left): Passing an old Cornish cottage at Luxulyan on 16th April 1985 with a Goonbarrow Junction to Carne Point, Fowey, train of Clay Hoods are Nos. 37181 and 37247. In recent years the use of two Class 37s on heavily-loaded china clay trains has become relatively commonplace, especially on the workings to and from ECC Rocks. Luxulyan Station lost its goods yard and passing loop status many years ago.

J. Vaughan

Plate 58 (Above): Peter Hamley is one of Goonbarrow Junction's two regular signalmen. Peter, a former Southern Railway employee, was transferred to Goonbarrow from Bodmin Road signal box after the Bodmin General to Wenford Bridge line closed. In spite of sometimes difficult conditions outside, the interior is, in the best traditions, kept immaculate, with floor swept and brasses polished. The next signal box in the 'up' direction is now St. Blazey and on the 'down', St. Dennis Junction.

J. Vaughan

Plate 59 (Right): About four china clay trains per day visit ECC Rocks at Goonbarrow which, except for the rare workings to Carbis Wharf, is now the only source of china clay traffic in the immediate area. On 28th February 1984, No. 37185 is about to indulge in a little shunting.

J. Vaughan

Plate 60: Most of the steeply graded 3½ mile long Goonbarrow branch was closed during 1965, and any traffic coming from the many minor china clay dries was either terminated or conveyed by other means. The freight service had by then dwindled to but one train per day. When photographed some 20 years after closure, the preservationists had moved in at the Imperial dries, south of Bugle. This line-up includes a GWR wagon of 1924 vintage. Note the disused clay dry chimneys.

J. Vaughan

Plate 63 (Right): A rare photograph of a train working the Goonbarrow branch in the late 1950s. One of the intermediate sidings is shunted by 1600 class 0-6-0 pannier tank No. 1626. The locomotive has white wheel rims from shunting the china clay sidings, and note the complete absence of brake pipes on the clay wagons. These were vacuum-fitted from about 1970.

C. H. A. Townley

Plate 61: Imperial No. 1 clay dries on 17th May 1984 — the attractive site now occupied by the Cornish Steam Locomotive Preservation Society. This is not an open site but open days are held from time to time and the main exhibit is the Par Harbour locomotive with cut-down cab — *Alfred* — as already featured in this volume. There is little else to see on the abandoned line.

J. Vaughan

Plate 62: This photograph shows the futility of trying to trace some old lines of the Cornwall Minerals Railway. This is the view of the bridge which spans the A391 St. Austell to Bugle road, near Carthew. In no time at all, either nature has reclaimed its land or new clay workings have obliterated most of the signs of where the branch trains trundled (*see also Plate 148*).

J. Vaughan

Dennis follows the route of the former canal and tramway. After Middleway Bridge Crossing, the single line crosses the main Liskeard to St. Austell road and continues to the still active clay works at Ponts Mill, which is featured elsewhere. A Class 08 shunter propels wagons to Ponts Mill as required but there can be several days between trains. The line from Ponts Mill to the small station at Luxulyan has a ruling gradient of 1 in 40 with a maximum incline of 1 in 37. The Luxulyan Valley is rich in mining and railway history and relics can be found in abundance deep in the undergrowth. The greatest relic is the massive Treffry Viaduct/Aqueduct built in the late 1840s and which stands majestically nearly 100ft. above the ground. It is still possible to walk across the structure and look down on the Newquay branch.

The line passes through a deep rock cutting and past Luxulyan station (once known as Bridges) to reach the passing loop at Goonbarrow Junction, just short of Bugle station. Here the Goonbarrow branch left the Par to Newquay line. The branch was some 3½ miles in length and from the junction to Carbean Siding the gradient was a steady 1 in 39 for most of the way. The line was subject to severe locomotive restrictions and once the old CMR engines had gone the older classes of 0-6-0 pannier tank, followed by the 1600 class, were used. Special authority was needed for one of the 2-6-2 prairie tank locomotives to use the line. By the mid 1950s only one daily train ran over the branch calling as required, at the ten intermediate sidings on its return journey. The sidings gradually closed and most of the line succumbed on 29th April 1965. The line had included a 341yd. tunnel at Stenalees, a locomotive shed at the same point and a reversal point at Gunheath. One of the former sidings, English Clays' Imperial No 1, is now a preservation centre. The minor branch from Bugle to Wheal Rose, which also opened in 1893, was closed at the same time as the major part of Goonbarrow branch.

There is still plenty of clay train activity at Goonbarrow Junction with a substantial output from the massive ECC Rocks Works. In fact there is a BR 'handover' point where an ECC diesel shunter takes over. Rail traffic is despatched in many forms ranging from the evergreen Clay Hoods to the massive Polybulk wagons bound for Switzerland. The branch to Carbis Wharf survives and the track runs parallel to the Newquay branch to a point west of Bugle station. This line is used about once per month but at least it remains open. For many years trains for Carbis have been propelled to the wharf because there are now no run round facilities (*see plate 123*). Obviously all clay movements to the Goonbarrow area have to fit in with the passenger service on the Newquay branch but the only really busy time on the branch is on summer Saturdays when there are no clay trains.

There is now no clay traffic west of Bugle but that was certainly not the case in the past. St. Dennis Junction was a major traffic centre with both the Retew branch and the line from Burngullow radiating from the area. In the mid 1950s there were no less than 17 china clay sidings and two level crossings, between St. Dennis Junction and Burngullow, a distance of only 7 miles. Despite the fuss

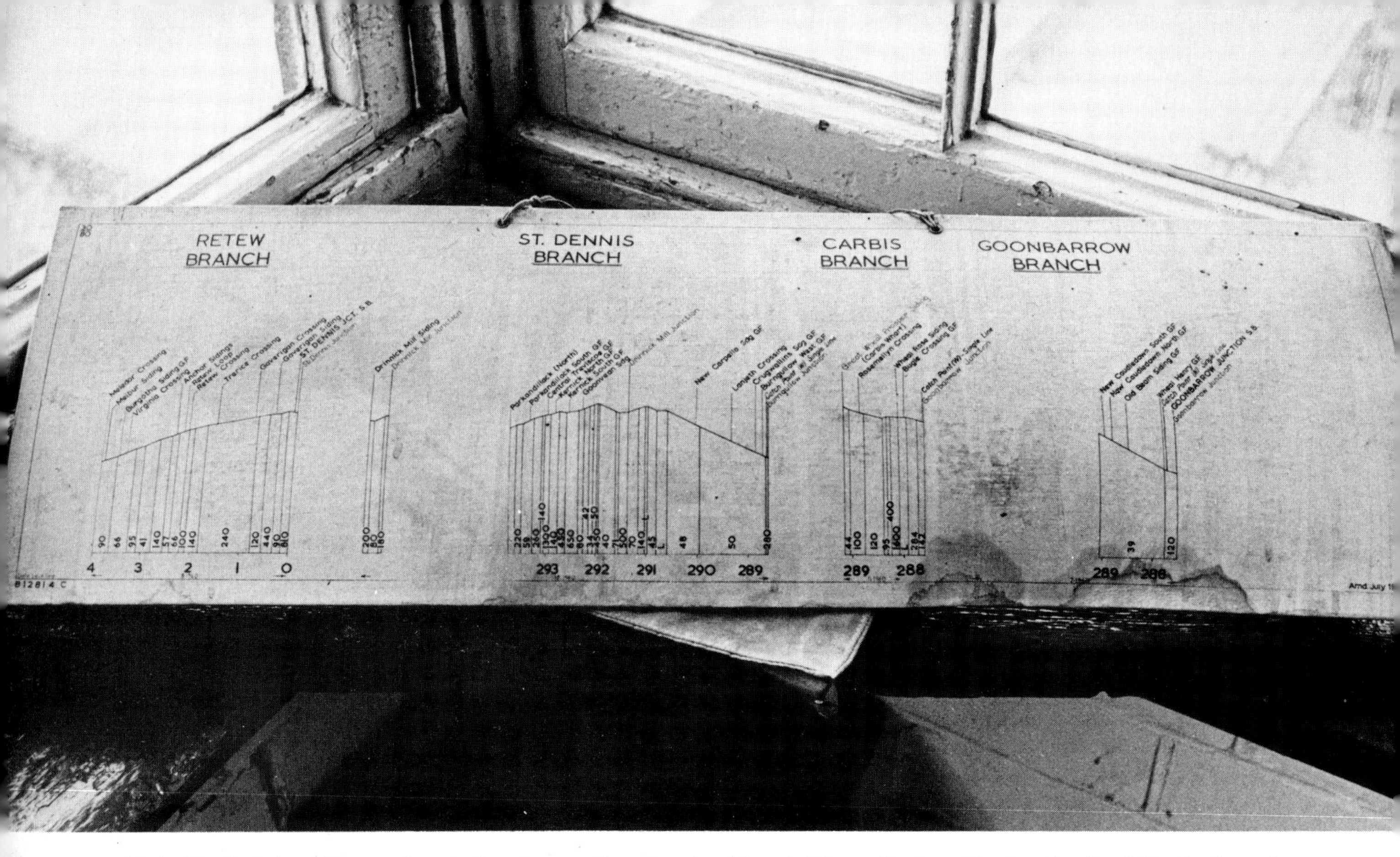

Plate 64: An interesting survivor in Goonbarrow Junction signal box is this gradient profile showing the following branches, with steepest gradient in brackets: Retew branch (1 in 41), St. Dennis branch (1 in 34), Carbis branch (1 in 44) and Goonbarrow branch (1 in 39). Interesting to relate is that although the major part of the Goonbarrow branch closed in 1965, this 1970-amended diagram shows the branch open, at least to New Caudledown, South ground frame. Only the St. Dennis and Carbis branches survive.

J. Vaughan

made about completing the link between the early tramway to Hendra and Drinnick Mill, very little use was made of a through running facility. There had been a difficulty until 1892 in that there was a change of gauge at Drinnick Mill but even in the 1950s there was only one through working per day. During 1966 the section from St. Dennis to Parkandillack Siding was closed and lifted, leaving just the 4½ miles up from Burngullow.

The Retew branch faired a little better. After extending the line to Meledor Mill from Melangoose in 1912 the branch prospered and a total of 10 sidings in the line's 4 miles length were provided. This branch was particularly attractive, passing through woodland scenery beside the stream which is the source of the River Fal. Trains worked on the 'pick up goods' principle and by the 1950s there were two round trips per day over the branch with some trains double headed. This branch gradually faded and after traffic had become very irregular the line simply petered out in the early 1980s. A railway enthusiast's special diesel multiple unit traversed the line in April 1977 and most of the track was lifted in 1983. Once these branches closed, St. Dennis Junction became a misnomer and now its only importance is as a passing loop on the Newquay branch and for a siding to a nearby spoil tip. There were masses of sidings in this and other areas and the list on page 41 from the year 1956 shows just some of the sidings used by the clay companies.

Plate 65 (Right): Trains to Carbis Wharf are always propelled because there are now no run-round facilities at the clay dries. The branch runs parallel with the Newquay branch from Goonbarrow Junction to the western side of Bugle Station — *see Plate 123.* To be more precise, the line serves the delightfully-named Great Wheal Prosper Clay Sidings. In this 1957 view, No. 1626 heads sister 0-6-0PT through Bugle Station with a load from Carbis.

C. H. A. Townley

ENGLISH CHINA CLAYS GROUP

Siding Name	*Approximate Position*
Bojea	St Austell
Burgotha	Meledor Mill
Burngullow West	Burngullow
Carbean	Bugle/Goonbarrow
Carloggas	Drinnick Mill
Caudledown	Bugle/Goonbarrow
Carlyon Farm	St. Austell
Carnsmerry	Bugle/Goonbarrow
Cornish Kaolin	Burngullow
Crugwallins	Burngullow
Dubbers No. 1 & 2	Drinnick Mill
Great Treviscoe	Drinnick Mill
Grove	Meledor Mill
Gunheath	Bugle/Goonbarrow
Hallivet	Bugle/Goonbarrow
Imperial	Bugle/Goonbarrow
Kernick	Drinnick Mill
Little Treviscoe	Drinnick Mill
McLarens	Melangoose Mill
Martins New	Bugle/Goonbarrow
Melbur	Meledor Mill
Methrose	Burngullow
New Caudledown	Bugle/Goonbarrow
New Gunheath	Bugle/Goonbarrow
New Halwyn	Melangoose Mill
New Meledor	Meledor Mill
New Trerice	Melangoose Mill
Oil	Bugle/Goonbarrow
Old Beam	Bugle/Goonbarrow
Par Harbour	Par
Parkandillack	Parkandillack
Parkyn and Peter's	Burngullow
Ponts Mill	St. Blazey
Rocks	Bugle/Goonbarrow
Rosevear	Bugle/Goonbarrow
Stannon	Wenford Bridge
Stone Wharf	Drinnick Mill
Tolbenny	Meledor Mill
Trelaver	Drinnick Mill
Trevanny	St. Blazey
Treviscoe	Drinnick Mill
Virginia	Meledor Mill
West Goonbarrow	Bugle/Goonbarrow
West of England New	Drinnick Mill
West of England	Burngullow
West Treviscoe	Meledor Mill
Wheal Anna	Bugle/Goonbarrow
Wheal Henry	Bugle/Burngullow
Wheal Rose	Bugle/Goonbarrow

Other sidings for clay train usage were at Bodmin Road, St. Blazey, Doublebois, Burngullow, Heathfield (Devon), Sutton and Cattewater Harbours (Plymouth, Devon), Liskeard, Moorswater, St. Austell, Wenford Bridge and Leith (Scotland). Other companies then owned:

Carbis Wharf	Bugle/Goonbarrow
Goonvean	Drinnick Mill
Goonvean (same)	Par
Restowrack	Drinnick Mill
Carne Point	Fowey
Marsh Mills	Plymouth (Devon)
Heathfield (Devon)	Newton Abbot
Marland (Devon)	Torrington
Meeth (Devon)	Torrington
Lansalson	St Austell
Fal Valley	Melangoose Mill
Retew	Melangoose Mill
South Fraddon	Melangoose Mill
Trelavour	Parkandillack
Trerice	Melangoose Mill
Trenance	St Austell
Onslow	Bodmin Road
Treskilling	Luxulyan
St. Dennis and Parkandillack	Drinnick Mill
Lukes New and Old	Drinnick Mill
Varcoes and Sales	Drinnick Mill and Bugle
Whitegate	Drinnick Mill
New Carpella	Burngullow
Old Carpella	Drinnick Mil
Beacon Clays	Burngullow

and many others . . . (some of the above were later taken over by ECC).

Plate 66: It seems remarkable that there is now no china clay activity on the railways west of Bugle. In years gone by, St. Dennis Junction, seen here, was the hub of a wheel, with clay coming up the Retew branch from Meledor Mill, from the line to Drinnick (and through to Burngullow), to Newquay for shipment, and via Bugle to Par and Fowey. Now St. Dennis Junction is merely a passing loop on the Newquay branch and a spoil tip. Here No. 5519 has just come off the Retew branch, and No. 4294 waits beside a toad brake on the main line.

C. H. A. Townley

Plate 69 (Right): Well over 700 Class 5700 0-6-0 pannier tanks were built, and they could be found all over the GWR and WR systems. Cornwall was no exception and when photographed with the traditional toad brake van on 11th July 1955, it was No. 3635 which was working the Retew branch at Meledor Mill. Note the old style uniform of the railwayman and the white pyramid peeping over the top of the distant hill.

R. C. Riley

Plate 67: A real Great Western scene, but in BR days. Passing Virginia Crossing on the Retew line is 2-6-2 Prairie tank No. 5519, bringing 100 tons of clay in eight Clay Tip wagons up from Meledor. Traffic gradually dwindled, and although the line was served by many intermediate sidings, they had all fallen into disuse by about 1980. The branch was just over four miles long.

C. H. A. Townley

Plate 70 (Right): After a morning run down from St. Dennis Junction, No. 3635, one of the ubiquitous 5700 class of pannier tanks, arrives at Meledor Mill. When this photograph was taken on 25th July 1960, the track was already overgrown, and yet traffic continued for another 20 years. The entire scene is now only a memory, but fortunately a memory captured on film.

M. Pope

Plate 68: Although the Retew branch was opened by the CMR in 1874, it was not until 1912 that the line was extended from Retew to Meledor Mill. In the latter days, Meledor produced much of the rail-borne traffic, but this was later transferred to the roads when the line closed. When photographed in 1957, there were two trains per day over the branch and occasionally trains were double-headed. Here, 1927-built 4500 class locomotive No. 5519 shunts Meledor.

C. H. A. Townley

DRINNICK MILL AND PARKANDILLACK

In 1869 the Newquay and Cornwall Junction Railway sponsored the building of a line from Burngullow to Drinnick Mill and Hendra which was in a strategically important position for the china clay industry. The line was to connect with the Cornwall Railway's main line at Burngullow and therefore the branch was laid to the 7ft. broad gauge. As mentioned elsewhere, by the time the track was laid to Drinnick Mill the group ran out of cash and it was not until 1874 that the CMR connected this line with the tramway which ran to Hendra, near Parkandillack. There was an inconvenient change of gauge at Drinnick Mill until the broad gauge was abandoned in 1892. The northern part of the line was eventually laid to mixed gauge but this was just to satisfy legal requirements and the broad gauge traffic never ran north of Drinnick Mill.

Many sidings sprouted off of this line and Drinnick was a major centre with a coal-fired power station operated by ECC that provided much of the power used within the china clay industry. The power station is still in limited use and the rail discharge point at ECC Drinnick, is now Cornwall's only coal concentration depot to also serve the local coal merchants. The coal arrives in modern HEA wagons as part of the mainly china clay ABS freights. The line never had a passenger service and yet Drinnick Mill had a station master. Gradually the northern section from Parkandillack to St. Dennis fell into disuse and it was formally closed in 1966. This closure focussed attention on the 4½ miles up from Burngullow, and to cope with modern loads and 80 tonne capacity wagons, much of the track was upgraded. There are still several clay works open along the line and up to four trains per day visit the branch. To reach the Drinnick Mill clay works trains must reverse at Nanpean Wharf (where calcified seaweed is sometimes loaded into special "Tiger" wagons) and normally only Clay-Hoods are loaded there. Most traffic now comes from Kernick, Treviscoe, Trelavour and especially Parkandillack. This is the starting point for the long distance air-braked freights.

The signalbox at Drinnick has gone but the goods office in the 'V' of the junction above Drinnick Mill is open for one shift per day and at the time of writing it is still gas-lit. Until October 1986, movements were controlled by Burngullow signalbox on the main line and large type 4 diesels share the duties with type 3 Class 37s. At the northern end, the line runs through 'moonscape' china clay country and armed with an ordanance survey map it is well worth a visit.

Plate 71 (Below): Pride of the erstwhile Cornish Railways was No. 37207 *William Cookworthy* which was normally kept in reasonable external condition. The locomotive is heading a morning air-braked service off the Drinnick Mill and Parkandillack branch at Burngullow. The main line is in the left foreground and, until 1931, there was a junction station. However, the branch has never had a passenger service on its entire 114 year history.
J. Vaughan

Plate 72 (Above Right): A totally Cornish scene on the southern fringe of the Hensbarrow Down area at Lanjeth. Passing a most splendid lineside cottage with a massive 54 wagon 1,080 tonne (gross) load of china clay from Kernick and Treviscoe dries, on 3rd October 1985, are Nos. 37222 and 37196 *Tre Pol and Pen.* The entire ensemble is destined for Carne Point, Fowey. Here the brakes will be on for the steep descent although the 3,500hp produced by the duo will be required for the hard climb up to Treverrin Tunnel.
J. Vaughan

Plate 73 (Below Right): The Class 25s worked hard on the china clay branches between 1971 and 1980 but with the arrival of the first Class 37s in 1978, their future in Cornwall was doomed. The Class 25s were, at 1,250hp, underpowered, for some of the clay workings and trains were sometimes double-headed. Here a brace of 'rats' pause at Drinnick Mill Junction in 1976 before proceeding to St. Blazey.
English China Clays/R. Dovey

0000

Plate 74 (Above): On 18th April 1985, the afternoon ABS working from St. Blazey to Parkandillack comprised just a single Cargowaggon. With typical china clay country scenery behind, No. 45072, one of the heavy 1-Co-Co-1 'Peak' class locomotives leaves Drinnick Mill, driven by a St. Blazey crew, and with resident shunter Ivor Trudgeon visible through the central cab window.

J. Vaughan

Plate 75 (Left): On 11th June 1981, nearly a year before it was named *William Cookworthy,* No. 37207 shunts Clay Hoods at Drinnick Mill. Few clay trains visit these dries at the time of writing although from March 1985 coal wagons were unloaded there for local distribution. The 105 tonne locomotive looks rather hefty for the lightly-laid track and rotting sleepers. China clay has been produced in this area for nearly 200 years and the railway has made its contribution for over a century.

J. Vaughan

Plate 76 (Above Right): By contrast, the track here between Drinnick Mill Junction and Treviscoe, is modern welded flat-bottomed rail on concrete sleepers. On a very wet 20th April 1983, No. 37181 returns from Parkandillack with four 'Tiger' wagons forming the 14.30 Parkandillack to Severn Tunnel Junction. On the right is the now abandoned Goonvean and Restowrack Siding, the junction of which can be detected behind the last wagon of the train.

J. Vaughan

Plate 77 (Right): With old clay tips as a backcloth, No. 37135 driven by Driver Bonney of St. Blazey, recovers a single wagon of china stone from Goonvean Siding, near Treviscoe. The siding, owned by the Goonvean and Restowrack Clay Co., closed in 1984. This entire area is littered with the remains of past mining activity, and sadly many of the detailed changes were never chronicled. However, in railway terms, many of the dates of significant developments have been collated and recorded in this volume.

J. Vaughan

37135

Plate 78 (Left): On 14th June 1984, the photographer did well to record a very relevant Class 47 in action at Kernick Dries, Treviscoe, on china clay duties. No. 47076 *City of Truro* was subsequently converted to Class 47/4 with electrical train heating, renumbered No. 47625 and put to work primarily on main line passenger duties.

R. Fuller

Plate 80 (Right): At the end of the 4½ mile stretch of line from Burngullow is the massive ECC Parkandillack (sometimes spelt Parkandillick) Works, and also the Goonvean Company's Trelavour Siding. Much of Cornwall's long haul china clay traffic originates here, including the two daily ABS 'Speedlink' services to Severn Tunnel Junction, and beyond. On 4th October 1985, Class 50 No. 50018 *Resolution* had a suspect traction motor and it had been assigned to china clay duties, providing a fairly unusual sight. The 2,700hp main liner prepares to get a 400 tonne load underway.

J. Vaughan

Plate 81: Penetrating deep into china clay country and surrounded by white pyramids are No. 37247 and 37181 as they make their way down the Drinnick Mill branch on their way from Carne Point to Kernick Dries on 19th April 1985. The pair are passing the abandoned Goonvean Siding, featured in *Plate 77,* where the occasional wagon of china stone was once loaded.

J. Vaughan

Plate 79 (Left): By the mid-1950s, only one train per day worked right through from St. Dennis Junction to Burngullow on the Cornish main line. Consequently, other than for the railway map, it was no great loss when the St. Dennis to Parkandillack section was closed in 1966, leaving just the 4½ miles from Burngullow to Parkandillack in situ. This section is well-used and the photograph shows the present terminus on 16th May 1984. Shunter Ivor Trudgeon couples 'Peak' Class 46 No. 46027 (now scrapped) to a TGV Ferrywagon, while, on the left, is the line which once continued to St. Dennis Junction.

J. Vaughan

MARSH MILLS

Plate 82: Marsh Mills is located to the north of Tavistock Junction, about a mile east of Laira. It is one of Devon's heaviest producers of china clay for shipment by rail. The works was opened during 1921 and rail connected by a steeply-graded spur off the branch line to Tavistock. The clay is piped from parts of Dartmoor and one pipeline follows part of the course of the abandoned Lee Moor Tramway. The works has always had its own motive power for shunting, and in this 1958 view both an 0-4-0 Fowler and a 'fireless' locomotive are visible.

C. H. A Townley

Plate 83: A Class 08 shunter brings wagons from Tavistock Junction to a hand-over point where an ECC English Electric 0-4-0 shunter now takes over. Seen from the weighbridge, the shunter arrives with a single 'Tiger' bogie wagon off the 'down' morning train from Severn Tunnel. Output by rail varies enormously, and while this was the only wagon dealt with on this day, the following two days would see 22 Polybulk wagons loaded for a Swiss customer.

J. Vaughan

Plate 85 (Right): This photograph is full of interest. No. 08953 *Plymouth* has just collected a single 80 tonne 'Tiger' wagon from Marsh Mills and it is standing at what was once Marsh Mills Station while the shunter closes the crossing gates. The works can be seen in the background towering above the rural scene. The Plym Valley preservation group have their stock on sidings just out of sight, centre left. Note the shunter's pole on the buffer beam.

J. Vaughan

Plate 84: On 18th May 1984, the English Electric shunter waits for an articulated lorry to be loaded before entering the dries with a 'Tiger' wagon, which will be loaded with 57 tonnes of pelletised clay. It will then be worked down the branch to the closed Marsh Mills Station and be collected by a BR Class 08 shunter. It pays to photograph china clay works in dull weather because sunshine on the white clay can produce uncontrollable contrast.

J. Vaughan

STOP
Open crossing gates before proceeding

BALL CLAY

Plate 86 (Left): Although this book specifically relates to china clay trains, a few pictures of ball clay trains have been included. In December 1971, during the last fortnight of passenger operations on the Swanage branch in Dorset, a push-pull Class 33/1 hauls empty ball clay wagons past Worgret Junction near Wareham, down to Furzebrook for loading. The last clay train to use the line was in 1982.

J. Vaughan

Between Wareham and Swanage, on Dorset's Isle of Purbeck, two tramways were opened during the nineteenth century. Pike Bros. Railway was built to 2ft. 8½in. gauge and originally ran from pits around West Creech to the shore of Poole Harbour. From 1884, exchange sidings with the L&SWR Swanage branch were provided. The line closed in stages, but finally in 1957. The other line was the Goathorn Railway, also known as Fayles Tramway, which comprised two 3ft. 9in. lines to transport clay from the Norden area, also to Poole Harbour for transhipment to barge. This very old line was regauged to 1ft. 11½in. in 1948. The earliest section closed in 1905 and it finally succumbed between 1969 and 1972. Ball clay continued to be transported from Furzebrook Sidings until 1982, then under the auspices of English China Clays.

Plate 87 (Below): Nowadays, clay train workings on Saturdays are a little unusual. After receiving a tip that at 06.00 hours a Class 37 would be travelling from St. Blazey to Newton Abbot to pick up some ball Clay Hoods from the Heathfield line, a visit was made to Trerulefoot in East Cornwall to photograph the return working. Shortly after 09.00 on 5th April 1986 No. 37196 *Tre Pol and Pen* rumbled westward with its load, bound initially for Lostwithiel.

J. Vaughan

Plate 88 (Right): It is possible to tell the difference between china and ball Clay Hoods by the narrow yellow line on the ball clay covers. The line is just visible on the bottom of the cover of the leading Clay Hood. When photographed on 10th August 1983, one of the long-lamented Class 45 'Peaks', No. 45074, had just reversed its load into the 'down' sidings at Lostwithiel. There is time for a natter before the 136 ton locomotive goes about its next diagram.

J. Vaughan

Plate 89 (Below): Another sizeable area for ball clay production is around the Petrockstow Basin. For years clay trains worked down to Meeth and Marland and, in this 1977 view, a Class 25 diesel is about to leave Barnstaple Junction with clay empties. Sadly, the line to Bideford and Torrington closed to passengers in October 1965 and finally on 6th November 1982.

J. Vaughan

Plate 90: Although passenger services on the Newton Abbot to Moretonhampstead branch were withdrawn back in 1959, part of the line soldiers on for freigh traffic — mainly oil and clay. On 16th November 1983, the branch locomotive for the day was Class 31 No. 31286. Here it is marshalling in New Yard, Newton Abbot, before departure for Heathfield.

Charles F. Beatson

Plate 91: At the time of writing, clay loaded into the modern air-braked vehicles leaves the West Country in the two 'up' air-braked services which run, initially, to Severn Tunnel Junction on Mondays to Fridays. However, china and ball clay loaded into the little wooden-sided Clay Hoods is normally transported to Fowey. On 10th February 1981, No. 08954 shunts Heathfield Dries.

Charles F. Beatson

Plate 92: On 13th November 1982, part of the 'Speedlink' consignment was halted here at Teignbridge Gates due to flash floods the previous day, undermining the track. No. 31128 and two loaded 'Tiger' wagons wait for the permanent way gangs to remedy the problem. These French-built wagons arrived on the china clay scene during 1982 and almost overnight the little vacuum-braked 4-wheelers were withdrawn from the Potteries traffic.
Charles F. Beatson

Plate 93: Whereas the line from Barnstaple to Torrington and Meeth, and Ivybridge Sidings have all closed, and the Lee Moor Tramway has been long abandoned, it is now only Marsh Mills and the Heathfield branch which directly contribute to china clay trains in Devon. Rumbling down the branch towards Newton Abbot is No. 08954 with the two main freight commodities — clay and oil.
Charles F. Beatson

CHINA CLAY WAGONS

J. Vaughan

Plate 94: BR Railfreight VAB 45 tonnes gross loaded weight.

Plate 95: BR UCV 20 tonnes gross loaded weight.

Plate 96: BR Railfreight VDA 40.8 tonnes gross loaded weight.

Plate 97: Railease PRA 38 tonnes gross loaded weight.

Plate 98: BR Railfreight VGA 46.4 tonnes gross loaded weight.

Plate 99: STS TTA Slurry Tanker 45 tonnes gross loaded weight.

Plate 100: Tiger Railcar Leasing PBA 80 tonnes gross loaded weight.

Plate 101: Tiger Railcar Leasing PAA 51 tonnes gross loaded weight.

Plate 102: Traffic Services Polybulk 80 tonnes gross loaded weight.

Plate 103: Tiger Railcar Leasing Railiner 41 tonnes gross loaded weight.

Plate 104: SNCF Transferry Wagon 80 tonnes gross loaded weight.

Plate 105: Transfesa Holland 40 tonnes gross loaded weight.

Plate 106: European Cargowaggon 80 tonnes gross loaded weight.

Plate 107: Crossfield TCA slurry tanker 80 tonnes gross loaded weight.

ECC International
TIGER

TRL
Tullis Russell
The Papermakers

TRAFFIC SERVICES LTD

TRL
RAILINER
TRL

TRANSFERRY

CARGOWAGGON

TCA

Plate 108: In the mid-1960s, the advantages of transporting china clay in slurry form were evaluated and, during 1966, experiments were conducted whereby liquid clay was transported from Cornwall to North Kent. The advantages were many in that ECC did not need to spend time and money drying and refining the clay; it was easily loaded into rail tankers and the customer did not need expensive mixing equipment before using it. The risk of contamination was also eliminated. On 23rd February 1967, the inaugural 'Clayfreighter' service left St. Blazey for Sittingbourne in North Kent, behind No. D1670 (later No. 47085) *Mammoth.*
English China Clays/J. Vaughan

THE 'CLAYFREIGHTER'

CORNWALL TO KENT

Plate 109: The plan was for 18 slurry tankers to be supplied to Bowater's by Storage and Transport Systems Ltd. The service would run once per week, leaving Burngullow late afternoon on Thursday and arriving at Sittingbourne early on Friday morning, with the empties returning overnight on Mondays to arrive in Cornwall on Tuesday. No. D4000 (later No. 08832) shunts the gleaming new wagons at Burngullow in 1967. Note the '84B' St. Blazey shed allocation plate in the centre of the shunter's front end. The name "Clayfreighter" was dropped within a few weeks of commencement of service.
English China Clays/J. Vaughan

Plate 110: On 11th June 1981, No. 47094 leaves the mighty Blackpool Works behind and heads for St. Austell. At this time the 'up' 'Clayfreighter' was booked to leave Burngullow at 19.45 as train 6041 THO, returning at 04.26 as train 6V65 TO. Theoretically, in terms of frequency and hours of darkness, the train was difficult to photograph, but as it sometimes ran early or late, a chance photograph was possible. For example this train had just left Burngullow — some two hours early.

J. Vaughan

Plate 111: Class 47s always reigned supreme on the Bowater's train. Nevertheless, on 20th May 1976, there was some welcome variety when 'Western' Class 52 No. D1051 *Western Ambassador* growled up the Fowey Valley between Bodmin Road (now Parkway) and Doublebois, with over 500 tonnes of clay slurry for the North Kent paper mills (but with a gross trailing weight of over 800 tonnes).

J. Vaughan

Plate 112: Although based on 1984 timings, these empty TTA tankers should have left Sittingbourne at 19.25 on Monday night (arriving Burngullow at 03.30 Tuesday). They were already over twelve hours late when photographed at Cullompton on Tuesday, 3rd July 1984. Heading south-west through Devon is No. 47150. Other customers now take their china clay in slurry form, such as Crossfield's of Warrington, who use large bogie tankers. In 1985, the train ceased to run when Bowater's relinquished their lease on the STS wagons, which now travel by 'Speedlink' Services as directed by the new hirers, ECC.

B. Morrison

Plate 113: It was several years after the event that I realised that on 26th January 1980 I had managed to photograph the Burngullow to Sittingbourne working in action at Waltham St. Lawrence, between Reading and Maidenhead. Obviously running many hours in arrears, No. 47051 was doing its best with a full load of eighteen STS tankers, each carrying 32 tonnes of china clay slurry but with a gross vehicle weight of 45 tonnes. The clay is used for both producing and coating paper.

J. Vaughan

Plate 114: Since 1976 there has been a need for English china clay for particular customers, originally in Italy and now in Switzerland. Once a fortnight a consignment of 1,200 tonnes is shipped to Dover in two trains which each comprise eleven loaded Polybulk wagons, containing 55 tonnes of clay per wagon (80 tonnes gross) with an all 'up' train weight of 880 tonnes. On 9th june 1980, part of a load was about to leave Goonbarrow behind No. 37299.

J. Vaughan

Plate 115: Late afternoon, in February 1984, finds a dull scene at St. Blazey, with the marker lights of No. 47283 glowing at the head of Polybulk wagons bound for Europe. Once on the Continent, two 11-wagon loads are joined, and the 22-wagon 1,760 tonne train makes its way from Dunkirk to the Swiss border at Basle. The service has been very efficient, with handling losses and contamination problems being eliminated.

J. Vaughan

Plate 116: In addition to Italy and Switzerland, a handful of Polybulk wagons loaded with china clay have been shipped to experimental destinations. Accordingly, when photographing a passing train, it is not possible to be sure of the destination. In this view Class 45/0 No. 45075 passes the site of Brent Station (for Kingsbridge) in 1982 with the morning St. Blazey to Severn Tunnel Junction working.

C. J. Marsden

Plate 117: Passing the golf course at Carylon Bay, near St. Austell, with the 14.30 Parkandillack to Severn Tunnel Junction working is 'Peak' Class 45/0 No. 45064, with a gross trailing weight of 240 tonnes in tow. The white china clay on the Polybulk wagons makes them stand out against the bleak winter landscape. The train will reverse twice to reach St. Blazey Yard.

J. Vaughan

Plate 118: One of the two fortnightly 11-wagon trains at Bristol (Temple Meads) on 31st August 1983 behind No. 47147. Even though the train is split for its travels on BR, it needs to be double-headed over the formidable South Devon banks as far as Newton Abbot. From there, one Type 4 is normally sufficient. This train is waiting for a path, following an IC125 High Speed Train.

J. Vaughan

Plate 119: Thundering up the climb to Box Middle Tunnel is No. 47089 *Amazon*, with the customary eleven Polybulks, on 13th May 1980. Inside the Polybulks, the china clay is stored in three separate compartments with a top load rapid discharge arrangement to avoid any spillage and prevent contamination. Unlike the old wagons, the Polybulks are entirely waterproof.

C. J. Marsden

Plate 120: The return journey from Switzerland to Cornwall is rather a different story because with an empty weight of only 23 tonnes each, all 22 wagons can be handled as a single train. Being fortnightly, the train cannot be anticipated, and on 16th January 1982 there was good fortune for the photographer, when on a chance visit to Clapham Junction, 'Crompton' Class 33/0 No. 33040 rumbled through from Dover with a full set of empties. A Class 508 electric multiple unit scuttles towards Waterloo.

J. Vaughan

Plate 121: There are no secrets from our intrepid photographic contributors and on 20th Feburary 1982 the Traffic Services clay-carrying Polybulks were even captured in Dover Western Docks being shunted on to the Sealink ferry by Nos. 09008 (left) and 09018 (right). Many of the large TGV and Ferrywagon vehicles also leave the country through the port of Dover.

Michael J. Collins

CARBIS WHARF

Plate 122: Great Wheel Prosper started life in 1830 as a tin mine but with Wheal Prosper they soon converted to china clay production when the price of tin suffered one of its many adverse price fluctuations. Great Wheal Prosper was one of the major installations on the north side of Hensbarrow Downs, but suffered by having to ship its clay to Charlestown Harbour in the south. The coming of the railway in 1874 almost halved the cost of transportation. The Goonvean and Restowrack China Clay Company have owned Great Wheal Prosper since 1937.

J. Vaughan

Plate 123: One of the little-used but presently still open lines is from Bugle to Great Wheal Prosper at Carbis Wharf. The line was opened in 1874. It is now owned by the small, progressive and long-established Goonvean and Restowrack China Clay Co. Ltd. About once per month an 80 tonne 'Tiger' wagon leaves here for Mossend, near Glasgow. However, on this day, a special train was photographed leaving the works hauled by No. 37207 *William Cookworthy.* The absence of run-round facilities means that all trains are propelled from Goonbarrow Junction. Note the weed-covered track and the virtual absence of ballast.

J. Vaughan

BODMIN ROAD TO WENFORD BRIDGE

The line to Wenford Bridge became a legend in its lifetime and it was with considerable sadness that the line was finally closed in 1983, less than a year short of its 150th anniversary. The history of the line has been written elsewhere but it is worth recording that the line from Wadebridge to Bodmin and on to Wenford Bridge was opened in 1834 and it became the first line in Cornwall to employ locomotives for continuous haulage. Some of the early locomotives on the line were notoriously unreliable which resulted in many humorous stories. The main line ran to Wenford with a spur line into Bodmin (later Bodmin North). The line was built to standard gauge so the designers had plenty of foresight. Although they had no physical connection with the Bodmin and Wadebridge line, the L&SWR purchased the concern as a tactical move to keep the rival Cornwall Railway (later GWR) out of North Cornwall. Ironically it was the GWR who opened up a branch from Bodmin Road to Bodmin General in 1887 and connected that branch to the Bodmin and Wadebridge line at Boscarne Junction in 1888. Thus after 54 years the B&W was connected to a main line. The L&SWR drove through their line from Halwill Junction, via Camelford in 1895 and at last the B&W was connected to its parent system. The line to Padstow was subsequently opened in 1899. The line from Boscarne Junction to Wenford Bridge never had a passenger train service.

China clay was carried on the line from 1862 and certainly until the GWR connected with the B&W, and possibly in later years china clay was shipped from the wharves at Wadebridge and Padstow. There was normally one train per day over the Wenford Bridge line but in the late 1930s the booming clay industry resulted in provision being made for a second train to run as necessary. The china clay sidings were 35 chains short of the Wenford Bridge terminus and clay was piped down from Stannon Moor some 6 miles from the clay dries. While clay prospered, other commodities dwindled and under the auspices of the Western Region of BR the L&SWR North Cornwall line closed in 1966 and in 1967 all passenger services between Bodmin Road, Bodmin General, Bodmin North, Boscarne Junction, Wadebridge and Padstow were withdrawn; a severe blow indeed. The line to Wadebridge remained open to freight until 1979 but then that too closed completely. Thus until that fateful day in September 1983 only the Bodmin Road to Wenford Bridge via Bodmin General and Boscarne Junction remained open, exclusively for china clay.

Once the 0298 class Beattie well-tanks had been retired and the 1366 class pannier tank successors had been withdrawn a Class 03 204h.p. shunter was tried for a short time in 1964, but a 350h.p. Class 08 from St. Blazey became the standard motive power. The normal practice was for the shunter to take empty wagons to the clay dries from either St. Blazey, Bodmin Road or Boscarne and to return with loaded wagons but to Boscarne only. It would then run light with its brake van to St. Blazey and a type 2 or 3 diesel would then trip the wagons from Boscarne to Bodmin Road (reversing at Bodmin General) where a load for Fowey would be made-up. The reason for this was that a Class 08 could haul only 8 loaded wagons up the climb from Boscarne to Bodmin General. The shunters occasionally brought up just 8 wagons if necessary. The service dropped to thrice weekly, as and when required, with sometimes lengthy gaps between trains. It was a quite unforgettable run up the valley of the River Camel and the train crews always had time for the locals or to spin a yarn to the stray enthusiast who had cadged a lift in the brake van. The Stannon dries had road access, the old track needed replacing and it was simply modern economics which resulted in closure in 1983.

Plate 124 (Below Left): In the last years of its existence the line from Bodmin Road (now Parkway) to Bodmin General, Boscarne Junction and the Stannon Clay Dries, near Wenford Bridge, was open only for the conveyance of china clay. Only Class 08 shunters worked through to Wenford Bridge but larger locomotives ran trip workings to Boscarne Junction to pick up loaded wagons left by the Class 08 shunter. On the murky evening of 10th June 1980, No. 37299 rolls off the line from Bodmin General to join the main line at Bodmin Road.

J. Vaughan

Plate 125 (Right): On 22nd July 1982, a total of thirty empty Clay Hoods were tripped from Lostwithiel to Boscarne Junction by No. 37206. With limited run-round facilities and only one other short siding, a complicated shunt was carried out to enable the Class 37 to run round its train at Bodmin General, seen here, in order to continue to Boscarne Junction. This line was opened by the GWR in 1887, but it lost its passenger service in 1967 and was closed completely in 1983. A preservation group has been formed to save the line.

J. Vaughan

Plate 126 (Below): On occasions, the Class 08 shunter would bring up to fifty wagons down from Wenford Bridge to Boscarne Junction, but due to the steep gradient, it was limited to eight loaded wagons from Boscarne to Bodmin General. Although the loaded wagons were usually recovered by larger locomotives, occasionally the shunter did bring up its maximum load. On 14th June 1978 Driver Hooper of St. Blazey keeps No. 08091 on the move with 180 tons in tow. Note that the wagons are not Clay Hoods.

J. Vaughan

Plate 127 (Left): Southern Railway locomotives on GWR metals. During 1963/4, Southern train crews from the SR outpost at Wadebridge worked their 'N' class Moguls through to Lostwithiel on china clay trains from Boscarne Junction. In this very rare picture taken on 5th May 1964, No. 31849 is banked up to Bodmin General by sister engine No. 31840 with a load of clay for Fowey.

S. C. Nash

Plate 130 (Right): Stannon Clay Dries, looking towards Wenford Bridge. Just a few months before closure, 1955 Derby-built Class 08 No. 08113 waits with 1954 Darlington-built brake van No. B952510, while the Clay Hoods are loaded in rather inclement weather. Although the dries may look the same as those featured in *Plate 21,* the wooden wheelbarrows were replaced by a large capacity front loading tractor and one wagon controller — just two men loading the train.

J. Vaughan

Plate 128 (Left): From Boscarne Junction to Wenford Bridge the character of the line changed as it followed the original 1834 route of the Bodmin and Wadebridge Railway. The Wenford section never had a passenger service and it was the privileged few who traversed the line and experienced the beautiful scenery alongside the River Camel. The permanent way was very lightly laid and tight radius curves could be found in abundance. Curving past the lifted siding at Tresarret is Class 08 No. 08091, with a load of empties.

J. Vaughan

Plate 131 (Right): For decades the Wenford Bridge line was famous for its steam motive power, because from 1893 to 1962 2-4-0 Beattie well tanks worked the line. In fact, the first 0298 class locomotive was shipped to Wadebridge because the line was not connected to the L&SWR until 1895. For 69 years the little tank engines eked out their days in this part of Cornwall, almost as if they had been exiled from the BR system. Here No. 30586 is seen in a beautiful setting, so typical of the line, with the 09.35 Wadebridge to Wenford Bridge freight on 17th May 1962, comprising three china clay wagons and a brake van.

S. C. Nash

Plate 129 (Left): At the end of the line's existence the service was thrice weekly as and when required. Sometimes several weeks passed without a train. A Class 08 would work out of St. Blazey Yard in the morning and run to Wenford, including reversing four times, shunting and waiting for the train to be loaded, before returning to St. Blazey in the afternoon. This would be a day's work for the train crew. The crew normally had their lunch in a Nissen hut at the Stannon Clay Dries. Here the guard on the left poses with Shunter Bill Richards and, on the right, Driver Albert Hooper. The Class 08 locomotive has since been scrapped.

J. Vaughan

30586

Stop
Cornish
Railways

Plate 132 (Above Left): China clay trains to and from Moorswater are sometimes few and far between and there is no regular pattern to the rail traffic. On 19th April 1983, there were two trains over the line. In this view, Class 37 No. 37181 trips the first of these up the Looe branch and underneath the 151ft. high Liskeard Viaduct on its way up to Liskeard. This steeply-graded connection from Coombe Junction, was built by the GWR in 1901 but the main line above dates back to 1859.

J. Vaughan

Plate 133 (Below Left): Driver Percy Wherry doesn't spare the horsepower as he gives 'Bill' (alias William Cookworthy — No. 37207) some notch seven treatment on the 1 in 40 climb from Coombe Junction to Liskeard with a modest 14 Clay Hoods in tow. This was one of two trips made from the works at Moorswater on 9th June 1986. The line on the left meanders down to the terminus at Looe.

J. Vaughan

Plate 134 (Above): During 1981 the diminutive Coombe Junction signal box and the lower quadrant semaphore signals were swept away. The freight loop on the right was lifted and shortly afterwards the Class 25s were transferred away thus a photograph taken as recently as 11th June 1980 is already history. Class 25 1,250hp No. 25225 makes for Moorswater with twenty empty Clay Hoods. The Class 25 was limited to fourteen loaded wagons on the return journey whereas a Class 37 can handle 22 wagons.

J. Vaughan

Far below the towering 150ft. high Moorswater Viaduct lies another interesting china clay installation, the Moorswater clay dries. This is yet another example where the production of china clay has been the sole reason for a section of railway line to remain in existence. In order to transport granite and tin ore from the highlands, comprising the Caradon Hills and the Cheesewring, down to Moorswater for transhipment onto barges on the Liskeard and Looe Union Canal, a railway was constructed. The standard gauge line was opened in 1844 to South Caradon and to the Cheesewring quarries in 1846. The line was extended around Caradon Hill in the 1880s. Mineral traffic increased and in 1860 an extension railway down to the port of Looe was opened, closely following the course of the canal which it eventually replaced. A passenger service to Looe started in 1879 but there was no connection with the Cornwall Railway (GWR) main line. In 1901 the GWR built a steeply graded link between the railways with the branch station at Liskeard having its own platform set at right angles to the main line station. Trains then ran through from Liskeard to Looe but a reversal was necessary at Coombe Junction, at the foot of the steep connecting line.

In the meantime the mineral business was crumbling and the lines north of Moorswater extending into the hills, were all closed in 1916. The GWR worked the remaining lines and absorbed the old companies. There was a branch locomotive shed at Moorswater and a little freight traffic but this fizzled out and the construction of the new Liskeard bypass road in the early 1970s resulted in the bulldozers moving in. A clay dry had been established in the valley in 1904 to treat the clay from Parsons Park on Bodmin Moor and this survived the aforementioned upheaval. In the early days, two thirds of the clay produced was shipped from Looe but this situation was short lived and gradually all the china clay was taken to the main line. Moorswater dries are now the sole reason for railway activity beyond Coombe Junction. The clay line once had its own siding from Coombe Junction signalbox but when the box was abolished in 1981 the passenger line was skewed, two ground frames were installed and the goods loop was lifted. However, it is still possible for a clay train to be locked in the section beyond the station, to the works, while the Looe branch diesel multiple unit goes about its business. There is a run round facility on the single track branch virtually under Moorswater Viaduct.

The works has good road access but china clay trains are still a regular feature of the movement to Fowey. Trains continue to trip to Liskeard where a single train is formed for the journey to the docks at Fowey. The reason is that even a Class 37 can haul only 22 loaded wagons up the gradient from Coombe Junction. The Class 25s were restricted to 14 wagons. There was once a large number of holding sidings at Liskeard but with much reduced freight traffic and IC125 platform lengthening, most have been lifted. Moorswater is something of a backwater but worthy of exploration, especially when a clay train runs.

Plate 135: On 5th July 1963, Class 22 No. D6320 (since scrapped) hauls a load of clay along the alignment of the old Looe & Caradon Railway between the Moorswater works and Coombe Junction. In the background is the impressive Moorswater Viaduct carrying the main line over the valley. This viaduct was rebuilt in 1881 and the piers of the original Cornwall Railway structure can still be seen. The alignment of the abandoned Liskeard & Looe Union Canal is in the centre of the photograph.

R. C. Riley

Plate 136: In years gone by, the railway on this Moorswater alignment continued up into the hills around Caradon and the Cheesewring. In 1902 the St. Neot Clay Company started to build its clay dries at Moorswater, and in 1904 the first load of china clay was taken by rail to Looe. A 200mm lens emphasises the scale of the 154ft. high Moorswater Viaduct which carries the main line over this pleasant little backwater. No. 37207 rumbles down the branch with the inevitable Clay Hoods.

J. Vaughan

Plate 137 (Right): A very pleasant and rural scene at Moorswater, in the valley below the viaduct carrying the main line. With the Moorswater clay dries in the background, No. 37135 leaves a rake of wagons for loading on 22nd February 1982. The clay is piped from the ECC Parsons Park Works a few miles away on the fringe of Bodmin Moor. All the clay loaded on to trains is despatched to Carne Point, Fowey, although many years ago some was shipped from the small harbour at Looe.

J. Vaughan

CLASS 50s ON CLAY HOODS

Plate 138 (Left): Ever since the 117 ton 100m.p.h. Class 50 locomotives arrived in the West Country in 1974, they have, from time to time, been employed on china clay duties. Appearances are infrequent but not rare. Capturing these main line locomotives on humble freight duty gives the photographer a sense of achievement. Curving past Kernick Clay Dries on the Parkandillack/Drinnick Mill branch is No. 50043 *Eagle* with twenty Clay Hoods for Lostwithiel.

J. Vaughan

Plate 141 (Right): A delightful sight in delightful weather. On 12th June 1986 two of St. Blazey's Class 37s were out of action and relief was provided by Plymouth (Laira) in the shape of No. 50043 *Eagle*. Making an unusual appearance at Treesmill at the head of 55 Clay Hoods travelling from Lostwithiel to Treviscoe, the immaculate Class 50 was very much at home. The locomotives are barred from some of the minor clay lines because of their restricted route availability.

J. Vaughan

Plate 139 (Left): On 4th October 1985, No. 50018 *Resolution* was restricted to local working and found its way from Laira to St. Blazey and then, alomost inevitably, it was employed on china clay duties. In this unusual scene the 'Hoover' is seen propelling a line of Clay Hoods from Blackpool Driers past the signal box at Burngullow to the now lifted 'up' siding west of the junction. The Drinnick Mill branch is above the rear cab.

J. Vaughan

Plate 142 (Right): Although there is a great deal of railway line west of Burngullow, this is now the western extremity of china clay train movements on the main line. With the massive Blackpool Clay Dries as a backcloth, No. 50001 *Dreadnought* makes for Drinnick Mill on 12th June 1978. Although this location is correctly called Burngullow, the Burngullow Clay Dries are about half a mile up the branch to Parkandillack.

J. Vaughan

Plate 140 (Left): This view of an old-liveried Class 50 on ball Clay Hoods dates back to 14th July 1981. Passing Exminster between Exeter and Dawlish is No. 50001 *Dreadnought* with half a dozen ball Clay Hoods from Torrington and china clay empties from Stoke-on-Trent. In the background is the M5 motorway. The semaphore signals have now been replaced under the Exeter mas scheme.

B. Morrison

50 001

CLASS 47s ON ABS

Plate 143: Class 47s have been employed on the many Cornish air-braked freight services since their introduction in the mid-1960s. However, the latest generation of air-braked vehicles mostly started life on china clay duties in the early 1980s. In recent times, the Class 37s have contained most of the local Clay Hood trips but the ABS trains to and from Severn Tunnel Junction and beyond have, in the main, been hauled by Class 47s or 'Peak' Class 45/46 locomotives. However, from 1st October 1985, the 1-Co-Co-1 'Peaks' were banned west of Bristol, and since then the Class 47s have reigned supreme. In the delightful valley beneath Restormel Castle, No. 47066 accelerates the 09.35 St. Blazey to Severn Tunnel working away from Lostwithiel, on 4th April 1986.

J. Vaughan

Plate 144: With a mixture of clay and cement wagons, No. 47223 thrashes up the climb from Par to Treverrin with the 15.28 St. Blazey to Severn Tunnel Junction working of 12th June 1986. The 280¾ milepost on the 'up' side is the mileage from Paddington via Bristol (Temple Meads) — the 'great way round' — and does not reflect the shorter 'cut-off' route via Castle Cary which was opened in 1906.

J. Vaughan

Plate 145: No. 47197 sweeps the afternoon St. Blazey to Plymouth (Friary) air brake freight across Bolitho Viaduct just east of Liskeard through typical East Cornwall scenery. Behind the locomotive is an 80 tonne ECC/'Tiger' bogie clay wagon, two 50 tonne Tullis Russell china clay wagons and six empty cement wagons travelling from Chacewater to Plymstock. The semaphore signal is Liskeard's 'down' outer home signal.

J. Vaughan

Plate 146: On 4th April 1986, an additional ABS from St. Blazey to Cliffe Vale, Stoke-on-Trent was necessary. Approaching Saltash at 18.25 is No. 47240 with the 560 tonne 17.35 ex-St. Blazey freight, comprising seven 'Tiger' Railcar Leasing PBA wagons. Not only is the train visible above the rooftops, but also one of HM warships, attached to the nearby Devonport naval base.

J. Vaughan

Plate 147: One of the many pitfalls which can fool the photographer of freight trains is the very loose adherence to the timetable. On 10th June 1986, the 15.28 St. Blazey to Severn Tunnel Junction working was photographed south of Treverrin Tunnel at 14.42! Passing the local agriculture is No. 47258 with a typically mixed load. The mixed traffic Class 47s have been workhorses in the Royal Duchy for over 20 years, and it seems that this situation is unlikely to change for some time.

J. Vaughan

ABANDONED CLAY LINES

Plate 148: While some three quarters of a million tonnes of china clay are moved by rail every year, the pipeline system is probably the most efficient conveyor. Over the years the use of pipelines has increased and some of the older china clay pits have become worked-out or have proved to be uneconomic. This has resulted in a number of line closures. This 1985 view shows the abandoned 341-yard Stenalees Tunnel on the Goonbarrow branch which was largely closed in 1965. It is still possible to walk through the tunnel.

J. Vaughan

Plate 149: The Trenance Valley line to Lansalson is another example of a closed clay line. It was opened after the Great War in 1920, was 1½ miles long, and had three intermediate sidings. It partially closed in 1964, then completely in 1968. After closure, the steeply-graded line also known as the Bojea branch, was soon taken over by nature and the site is now heavily overgrown. In this May 1984 photograph the disused works can just be seen, and the gaps for the rails in the foreground cobblestones can barely be detected. It is now hard to imagine the works in its heyday.

J. Vaughan

Plate 150: There were some ten china clay sidings leading to clay dries on the 4-mile Retew branch. A typical rail connected installation was South Fraddon Clay Dries, seen here. While the dates of some line and pit closures and other significant developments are recorded, over the years many aspects of the history of china clay trains and the dries they served have gone unrecorded. South Fraddon probably saw its last train in the late 1970s.

J. Vaughan

Plate 151: Tracing the old china clay lines is a fascinating activity. In some areas remains and relics can be found in abundance while at other locations there is absolutely no trace of a once thriving branch line. The old track (left centre), seen here, connected the dries of the Goonvean China Clay and Stone Works with the Drinnick Mill branch. Note the old weed-covered spoil heap in the background.

J. Vaughan

TANK ENGINES

Plate 152 (Left): Other than for a handful of main line trains, all china clay workings in the days of steam were handled by tank engines. Most of the locomotives were small 0-6-0 or 2-6-2 types, although there were some notable exceptions such as the 2-4-0 well tanks of the L&SWR and the large 2-8-0 and 2-8-2 tanks used mainly on the St. Blazey to Fowey line. In this view of the Newquay branch near Roche, the guard is pinning down the brakes of a clay train which is working back from St. Dennis Junction to St. Blazey. Double-heading the train are 4200 class 2-8-0 No. 4294 and 4500 class 2-6-2 No. 5519.

C. H. A. Townley

Plate 154 (Above): With the day's work all but over, Prairie tank No. 5521 and pannier No. 3655 are illuminated by the late afternoon sun as they glide downhill from Burngullow to Par Harbour with a load of china clay. They were photographed near Carlyon Bay Golf Course on 6th July 1955. Note the depressions in the wagon covers which held pools of water in wet weather. If pinholes appeared, the china clay could sometimes be contaminated, hence the development of the Clay Hood.

R. C. Riley

Plate 153 (Below Left): Lostwithiel change for Fowey reads the sign as 5700 class pannier tank No. 9755 passes the delightful gas lamps with 'up' clay empties on 23rd September 1960. This locomotive was one of St. Blazey's sizeable allocation of tank engines which were used almost exclusively for china clay workings on minor branch lines. By 1964 the steam era was at an end and although there are fewer clay trains nowadays, St. Blazey's motive power requirement has changed from 35 steam locomotives to 6 diesels.

R. C. Riley

Plate 155 (Below): These rails have long been lifted and nature has reclaimed all of this land (*see Plate 149*). Shunting at Lansalson on the Trenance Valley or Bojea branch in 1955 is 1906-built Churchward 4500 class 2-6-2T No.4552. The old dries on this line were gradually worked-out and the line closed completely in 1968. There was once a scheme to link this valley with the Pentewan Railway but the plans never came to fruition.

C. H. A. Townley

CLAY ON DEVON'S MAIN LINE

Whilst clay operations in Cornwall have been on a greater scale than in the County of Devon, the Devon rail routes have been a vital artery for the transportation of china clay. Many of the Cornish mineral lines were established before there was a rail link between Devon and Cornwall but once the Royal Albert Bridge was opened in 1859 it was inevitable that clay would be transported by rail to the Potteries in Staffordshire and beyond. Also once the Cornish ports were developed for clay-handling it was entirely predictable that loads would be taken from the Devon clay works to the Cornish outlets. Even in 1986 ball clay was still conveyed from Heathfield to Carne Point, Fowey in specially marked Clay Hoods. As mentioned elsewhere the clay from Dartmoor was handled by the Lee Moor tramway, the large Marsh Mills plant and a depot at Ivybridge. Other centres to the north of Newton Abbot on the old Moretonhampstead line and in the Petrockstow Basin in North Devon had their clay transported down branch lines to the main line for transhipment.

In the last two decades there has been a trend towards long distance clay hauls with privately owned or leased wagons. In addition to the traditional Potteries area and the Scottish paper mills, loads of high quality English china clay have been transported by rail and cross Channel ferry to Holland, France, Belgium, Spain, Italy, Switzerland and Germany. Large capacity wagons have been used such as the Polybulk, TGV Cargo and Ferrywagons already featured. These massive trains have had to cross the notorious South Devon banks and sometimes double headed type 4 diesel power has been necessary. There has been a trend to transport china clay in slurry form, with its many advantages for the user. The introduction of the 'Clayfreighter' in 1967 (a name subsequently dropped) for transporting slurry to Bowater's Mill at Sittingbourne in Kent and the large Crossfield bogie tanker wagons which work to Warrington are examples. Add to this the 'Clayliner' to Stoke-on-Trent (now included in the general ABS trains) and other clay trains and it is apparent that Devon's main line plays an important part in china clay transportation. With the recent modernisation of clay carrying wagons the new air-braked services can move at high speed and with good railway operations, enable guarantees on delivery to be made to customers with confidence.

Plate 156 (Below): The following sections trace the progress of china clay trains through the County of Devon to the Potteries of Staffordshire and the paper mills of Scotland. Having travelled over the South Devon banks, Class 47/0 No. 47091 emerges from Mutley Tunnel, Plymouth, with the 'down' 'Clayliner' empties from Stoke-on-Trent on 23rd July 1976. The train is passing the site of Plymouth (Mutley) Station which closed in July 1939.

J. Vaughan

Plate 157 (Above Right): Prior to the abolition of train headcodes in 1976, the photographer could identify particular trains such as 6M55, seen here. This Class 6 freight was bound for the London Midland Region, hence the '6' and the 'M', and is in fact the 18.10 St. Blazey to Stoke-on-Trent china clay train. This 1975 view shows 'Western' Class 52 No. D1052 *Western Viceroy* at Plymouth (North Road).

J. Vaughan

Plate 158 (Below Right): Contrasting with the previous photograph, is this modern air-braked china clay train forming the 15.15 St. Blazey to Severn Tunnel Junction working of 2nd March 1984. With two large Cargowaggons and a PRA 4-wheeler, No. 47283 is held 'centre road' at Plymouth (North Road). The train will depart at 16.27 for Tavistock Junction, Plymouth, where it will pick up more wagons and depart at 17.15.

J. Vaughan

M 55
D1052

5

Plate 159 (Left): Tottering up Hemerdon bank at less than 30m.p.h., on 24th July 1976, is Class 25/2 No. 25216 with clay empties for the loading point at Ivybridge. Although the siding at Ivybridge is still in situ, it is no longer used for china clay and the only Clay Hoods to pass this location nowadays is the occasional train to or from the Heathfield line at Newton Abbot.

J. Vaughan

Plate 160 (Left): Sweeping through Totnes with an 'up' mixed freight, on 4th August 1975. is 'Western' Class 52 No. D1055 *Western Advocate.* The leading two thirds of this vacuum-fitted freight comprises china clay wagons which will probably be remarshalled at either Hackney Yard, Newton Abbot or Riverside Yard, Exeter. The locomotive met its end in a crash near Worcester later that year and was cut up at Swindon in 1976.

B. Morrison

Plate 161 (Left): A regular and most welcome sight on the inter-regional china clay workings were the Class 45 and 46 1-Co-Co-1 'Peak' locomotives, although the Class 46 variety have all now been withdrawn from service. With an odd few oil tankers and cement wagons included the 'down' 'Clayliner' passes Totnes on 14th April 1981 behind Class 45/0 No. 45060 *Sherwood Forester.* The train is destined for Plymouth (Friary) Yard and then St. Blazey.

J. Vaughan

Plate 162 (Above): A scene from the 1950s finds 4-6-0 'Grange' class locomotive No. 6873 *Caradoc Grange* passing Laira Junction, Plymouth, with a load of clay from one of the South Devon works. Modernisation has completely transformed this location with track realignment, the demolition of signals and signal box, and the construction of a new road bridge. Just above the sixth wagon is where the Lee Moor Tramway crossed the main line.

R. C. Riley

Plate 163 (Right): It is hard to believe this is the site of the large junction station of Brent where once passengers changed for Kingsbridge. Only the disused signal box has survived as No. 37203 passes with 'down' Ball Clay Hoods. The ball clay will have come from Heathfield and will be travelling into Cornwall for shipment from the docks at Fowey.

C. J. Marsden

Plate 164 (Above): A glorious picture in glorious Devon. Toiling up the 1 in 37 towards the summit at Dainton Tunnel, on the afternoon of 2nd July 1979, is one of the real workhorses of the long-haul china clay train scene, 'Peak' Class 46 No. 46001 (now withdrawn). Although empty, the 60 wagons weigh well in excess of 400 tonnes and the 2,500hp Sulzer engine will be working hard.

B. Morrison

Plate 165 (Above Right): Although the situation will change drastically during the last few years of the present decade, Newton Abbot is a museum for the student of WR and GWR semaphore signalling. Passing between signal box and gantry on 25th September 1981 is No. 47248, with a rather short version of the 'down' 'Clayliner' from the Potteries. The train is vacuum-fitted and a brake van is not necessary.

C. J. Marsden

Plate 166 (Right): Just at the end of the holiday season and not a soul to be seen along the famous sea wall at Dawlish, although in poor weather with the sea apparently breaking over the promenade this may not be surprising! Four 80 tonne 'Tiger' wagons filled with china clay form the bulk of the 09.15 St. Blazey to Severn Tunnel Junction freight of 13th September 1983, seen passing behind Class 47/3 No. 47377.

C. J. Marsden

Plate 167: 'Hoover' power at Dawlish Warren on 24th June 1981, as Class 50 No. 50027 *Lion* hugs the South Devon coastline with the afternoon ABS from Severn Tunnel Junction. Six Railfreight VDA wagons used for bagged clay are mixed with four PAA wagons used by the papermakers, Tullis Russell of Markinch, Scotland.

C. J. Marsden

Plate 168: A panoramic view of Exeter (St. David's) Station, taken from the now demolished water tower (now the site of the new signalling centre). Setting out from Exeter (Riverside) Yard after a shunting interlude on 21st July 1977 is Class 47/0 No. 47136. Again the 'down' 'Clayliner' has been corrupted by the addition of other wagons in the centre of the train. All semaphore signals were replaced by colour lights during 1985.

B. Morrison

Plate 169: With the replacement of the wooden sided 4-wheelers on the long-distance clay runs, these little UCV/OOV wagons have been banished to the south-west, west of Newton Abbot. Thus this picture has become pure modern traction nostalgia and shows an old livery pre-naming view of No. 50040 (later *Leviathan*) rolling down from Whiteball Tunnel with the 'Clayliner' empties on 20th May 1978.

J. Vaughan

Plate 170: The electrical train heating facility on Class 45/1 No. 45107 will not be needed on this train despite the weather conditions. Having just passed from Somerset to Devon on 18th February 1978, the 'Peak' makes for Cornwall with the 04.24 Stoke-on-Trent to St. Blazey working. On the right is the now closed Whiteball Siding signal box.

J. Chalcraft

THE POTTERIES AND SCOTLAND

At one time the potters around Stoke-on-Trent in Staffordshire were the only users of large quantities of china clay. Once large deposits of china clay had been discovered in the South West, the wealthy owners took out leases on the clay pits but by the end of the 18th century the practical problems of running pits remotely with poor communications became apparent and the ownership reverted to the local landlords. That did not solve the transportation problems, with horses ploughing over rough terrain to reach inadequate harbours where sailing vessels conveyed small loads to the north west of England. The coming of the railways was to be their saviour as Par, Fowey and Pentewan were developed and rail connected transportation became cheaper and quicker and certainly more reliable. By the middle of the 19th century and the arrival of the Cornish main line, long haul clay trains were on the cards and photographs taken at the turn of the present century show railway wagons from pregrouping companies being used for clay distribution nationwide.

One of the most important trains, dubbed the 'Clayliner', regularly travelled from Staffordshire to Cornwall and vice versa. Until as recently as 1981 it still comprised little wooden bodied 12.5 tonne capacity vacuum braked wagons but something had to be done quickly as these short wheelbase vehicles were not commensurate with high speed Railfreight or Speedlink services. The little 4-wheelers even found themselves on the east and west coasts of Scotland, as the pictures show. The primitive wagon cover arrangements meant that china clay contamination was possible and rain could spoil the precious contents. Accordingly, by 1982 new 18.44 metre long air-braked Tiger wagons with a capacity of 57 tonnes and an all up weight of 80 tonnes were introduced and they replaced the 'Clayliner' by running as part of BR's Speedlink services. Many smaller air-braked, roller bearing wagons also entered the clay fleet in addition to large modern vehicles of the VTG Ferrywagon type from Europe. These modern vehicles now head north to Severn Tunnel Junction and on to Cliffe Vale (Stoke-on-Trent), Mossend (Glasgow), Corpach (Fort William), Markinch (Fife), Warrington, Harwich, Dover, Sittingbourne (Kent) and elsewhere. The photographs trace these workings with new and old wagons.

Plate 171 (Left): The elderly and rather primitive UCV clay wagons were speed restricted to 45 m.p.h. and the 'Clayliner' was booked to take over fourteen hours for its journey from Staffordshire to Cornwall. With the 3-link chain coupling swaying and the oil-lit tail lamp flickering, No. 46002 heads into the mist at Cogload Junction, north of Taunton, on 27th October 1979. This section of line has since been reduced to double track. The train is the 04.55 Etruria to St. Blazey working.

J. Vaughan

Plate 172 (Right): The track through Staplton Road to Filton was quadruple, but during 1984 the route was 'dequadrified'. In happier days a mixed freight traverses the route at Ashley Down and keeps to the Cardiff and South Wales lines while working to the Bristol area from Severn Tunnel Junction. The locomotive is No. 31320, the date is 26th May 1978 and the clay wagons can be clearly identified.

J. Chalcroft

Plate 173 (Right): The clay wagon content of this freight seems very meagre but is sufficient to justify a photograph of a pair of Class 20s on china clay duties. Passing Norton Junction, near Worcester, on 13th June 1980 with a Bescot (Birmingham) to Severn Tunnel Junction freight, are 'Choppers' Nos. 20192 and 20140. Once the outbound clay trains have been marshalled at Severn Tunnel the route to their many destinations can then vary enormously.

J. Chalcraft

Plate 174 (Below): About 5½ hours after leaving St. Blazey in Cornwall the 09.15 St. Blazey to Severn Tunnel Junction working rolls into its initial destination. The first three wagons will contain bagged clay and the four 'Tiger' wagons contain pelletised china clay. The latter will almost certainly end up at ECC's new depot at Cliffe Vale, Stoke-on-Trent — although a few make their way to Mossend, Glasgow. Photographed on 3rd August 1983, the motive power was 'Peak' Class 45/0 No. 45020.

J. Vaughan

Plate 175: Having traversed the old 'North and West' route through Hereford and Shrewsbury, this Stoke-bound clay train was photographed passing Nantwich on its way towards Crewe. Here, on 11th March 1982, Bescot's Class 47/3 No. 47337 was in charge of the 'white gold' from the hills around St. Austell.

P. A. Larke

Plate 176: On 28th August 1981, this heavy mixed freight, headed by 'Siphon' Class 37 No. 37138, contains a china clay portion as it approaches Gresty No. 2 signal box, near Crewe. The freight, the 7S98, is bound for Scotland and these clay wagons could well be destined for Fort William. Note the start of the 25kV overhead catenary.

P. Kynaston

Plate 177: One of the long-lamented Class 40 'Whistlers' on china clay duty at Gresty Lane, Crewe. On 12th October 1978 a very clean No. 40145, with central headcode panel, gets underway with a freight for Carlisle. This train will be routed over the Settle & Carlisle line.

P. Kynaston

Plate 178: This bright and crisp photograph shows a modern air-braked china clay train in the Birmingham area, while working from Cornwall to Stoke-on-Trent. 'Duff' Class 47/0 No. 47264 pulls out of the vast Bescot Yard with freight 6K30, the 10.30 Bescot to Cliffe Vale, on 27th April 1984, with at least seven 'Tiger' wagons in tow.

P. Kynaston

Plate 179: One of the most important destinations for china clay trains is Cliffe Vale, Stoke-on-Trent. Although only a small amount of the total china clay production is now used in china/porcelain/pottery, the Potteries area is still very important, especially in view of developments in the field of ceramics. On 17th May 1979, Class 08 shunter No. 08473 shunts clay wagons into the unloading area at Stoke-on-Trent.

A. O. Wynn

Plate 180: Approaching Treeton Junction, just south of Tinsley Yard, Sheffield, on 23rd July 1979 is No. 25270 with a mixed Toton to Tinsley freight, which includes china clay wagons. These wagons will almost certainly find their way over the Settle & Carlisle line to Scotland where the contents will be used in paper making.

J. Chalcraft

Plate 181 (Left): This Mossend, Glasgow to Arpley Yard, Warrington, freight runs daily Mondays to Fridays and it almost invariably contains china clay wagons. Now that the vacuum-braked UCVs have been withdrawn from the clay trade, all the wagons are air-braked, a prerequisite to join the 'Speedlink' system. On 9th April 1984, Class 86/0 No. 86009 passes Winnick Junction with a PRA and a 'Tiger' wagon clearly visible in the foreground.

J. Vaughan

Plate 184 (Right): A general view at Crianlarich Station in the West Highlands where the line to Oban diverges from the Fort William line. Passing, on 22nd June 1981, is No. 37021 with a china clay train from Cornwall bound for the Wiggins Teape establishment at Corpach, on the West Highland extension route to Mallaig.

J. Chalcraft

Plate 182 (Left): Photographs of the now extinct Class 06 shunters on china clay duty are rare. On 6th March 1980, Barclay diesel No. 06008 eases out of Markinch with a single china clay wagon and a load of coal en route to the Glenrothes Works of Tullis Russell. The old china clay wagons were replaced by the smart blue-liveried TRL-PAA air-braked wagons in 1982.

J. Chalcraft

Plate 185 (Right): In the heart of the West Highlands, at Tyndrum, is the 12.29 Mossend to Corpach ABS freight, headed by Class 37 No. 37190 on 14th June 1984. The third wagon from the rear is a PRA vehicle containing china clay. The train is near the famous Horseshoe Curve and the peak is that of Beinn Dorain.

J. Chalcraft

Plate 183 (Left): The wilds of the Settle & Carlisle line on a very bleak day. It seems remarkable that these wagons forming part of set No. 7459 will end up in Cornwall. Returning from Fort William in the West Highlands, freight 7VOO, the Carlisle to Severn Tunnel Junction, heads south between Shotlock and Moorcock tunnels behind No. 47089 *Amazon,* on 24th March 1982. The train was entirely comprised of UCV clay wagons.

J. Vaughan

Railfreight
37021

CLAY HOODS GOING AND COMING

Plate 186 (Left): The delightfully rural setting of Coombe Junction is typified in this morning backlit scene of an 'up' china clay train pausing at the diminutive halt. On the left, Vernon Collins walks towards No. 37235 after restoring the catch points which protect the Moorswater section from the diesel multiple unit which trundles from Liskeard to Looe and back, reversing at Coombe Junction on every journey. The sight of these delightful little Clay Hoods with their wooden bodies, 3-link chain coupling and single vacuum brake pipe will soon be a thing of the past.

J. Vaughan

Plate 187: Simply exuding power is this shot of 1,750hp, Class 37 No. 37247 assaulting the climb to Treverrin with 400 tonnes of china clay on 3rd October 1985. The dramatic late afternoon sun provides the backlighting while a 300mm Nikkor lens provides the impact. Since their introduction in Cornwall in 1978 the Class 37s have proved to be reliable and popular, with a route availability which enables them to traverse the majority of china clay lines and sidings.

J. Vaughan

CORNWALL'S MAIN LINE

Plate 188: Most of the minor china clay lines and branches have been featured in the previous sections but this feature shows the wide variety of clay trains and motive power to be found on the Cornish main line. Crossing Coombe Viaduct, Saltash, having just entered Cornwall from Devon on the Royal Albert Bridge in the background, is 'Peak' No. 45064 with the Severn Tunnel Junction to St. Blazey working of 28th February 1984. The train comprises five 'Tiger' wagons and two vans.

J. Vaughan

Plate 189: A delightfully mixed 15.15 St. Blazey to Severn Tunnel Junction working crosses the impressive Lynher Viaduct, near St. Germans on 19th April 1983, behind 135 tonne Class 45/0 No. 45040. The three leading vans contain paletted bagged china clay for the Netherlands, followed by three 'Tiger' wagons, a 'Clan' paper slurry tanker and two Tullis Russell wagons for Markinch.

J. Vaughan

Plate 190: In recent years there have been two long-distance china clay trains from the County of Cornwall on Mondays to Fridays. At one time they left St. Blazey at about 09.15 and 15.15 for Severn Tunnel Junction. However, in earlier days the main 'Clayliner' left St. Blazey at about 18.10 and all other traffic was formed in 'up' goods trains to Plymouth, Exeter or Newton Abbot. Leaving Liskeard on 2nd April 1979, is this St. Blazey to Newton Abbot freight headed by No. 37267.

J. Vaughan

Plate 191: A 'Peak' on Clay Hoods this far east of Lostwithiel is not an everday occurrence, but on 19th April 1983 a special Marsh Mills to Carne Point, Fowey, working produced Class 45/0 No. 45016. The 'Peak' is passing the now-demolished 'down' station buildings at Liskeard. The point on the left leads on to the Looe (and Moorswater) branch.

J. Vaughan

Plate 192: All of the sidings on the right have now been lifted following an IC125 platform extension project. These 'up' sidings at Liskeard were once very busy with a substantial goods shed located in the right background. They were subsequently used to store china clay and permanent way wagons. On 10th June 1981, the evening 'up' 'Clayliner' to the Potteries passes a rather damp Liskeard, behind No. 37142.

J. Vaughan

Plate 193: A cement tanker gets amongst the china clay vans on the morning Severn Tunnel freight of 11th August 1983. The train, hauled by No. 45078, is crossing St. Pinnock Viaduct — the highest in Cornwall — on single track, because in 1964, singling was deemed to be a cheaper alternative than the strengthening which would otherwise have been required.

J. Vaughan

Plate 194: New liveried Class 50s on china clay workings always make good pictures, firstly because such occurrences are rare, and secondly because it is something of an anachronism to see an e.t.h. 100m.p.h. express passenger locomotive on a humble clay train. Crossing the eerie East Largin Viaduct on a bleak 22nd February 1982, is No. 50041 *Bulwark* with a Liskeard (ex-Moorswater) to Lostwithiel clay train. Note the single track at this point.

J. Vaughan

Plate 195: The Fowey or Glynn Valley is quite magnificent with the railway line running along the hillside and passing over nine major viaducts, in a distance of about nine miles. From Bodmin Parkway, the line climbs for miles at gradients as severe as 1 in 57. There are splendid views from the train and for much of the distance there is a fine display of rhododendrons. No. 37297 made a splendid spectacle on St. Pinnock Viaduct on 1st March 1984 as it rolled down to Bodmin Parkway, with a load of clay from Moorswater.

J. Vaughan

Plate 196: While the artificially resident Forestry Commission conifers have taken over much of the Fowey Valley, in the area of Penadlake Viaduct the British deciduous trees have survived the challenge. Threading these trees in the heart of the valley is No. 47075 with the 09.15 ex-St. Blazey working of 10th August 1983. It is photographed through a 200mm Nikkor telephoto lens on a Nikon FM2 camera.

J. Vaughan

Plate 197: On its last legs, but struggling valiantly on a memorable evening in May 1976, is 'Western' Class 52 No. D1041 *Western Prince.* The sound of its two 12-cylinder, high revving, Maybach engines was quite superb as it edged up the valley east of Clinnick Viaduct. Within nine months, the magnificent 'Westerns' were extinct and diesel-hydraulic locomotives on BR were relegated to the annals of railway history. Fortunately No. D1041 was saved from the cutters torch and is privately preserved.

J. Vaughan

Plate 198: On 2nd June 1981, the substantial bulk of 'Peak' No. 45072 was employed on a Bodmin Road to Carne Point, Fowey, clay train and was captured on film near Restormel Castle, between Brownqueen Tunnel and Lostwithiel. With the closure of certain lines and installations, the only Clay Hood workings east of Lostwithiel are now to or from Moorswater, Marsh Mills or Heathfield/Newton Abbot.

J. Vaughan

Plate 199: This absolute gem of a china clay train was photographed at Bodmin Road on 13th December 1982. The shunter had just worked down from Wenford Bridge with a single wagon containing 13 tonnes of clay and a 20 ton brake van. Now the line has closed, the Class 08 No. 08113 has been scrapped and Bodmin Road Station has been renamed. Some call it progress!

J. Vaughan

Plate 200 (Above): Vintage modern traction days at Lostwithiel with a 'Whizzo' on china clay and 6-wheeled milk tankers in abundance. BR lost the milk contract and the Class 52s were withdrawn but the little clay wagons still clank and squeal their way around the area. On 19th May 1976, No. D1023 *Western Fusilier* brings a load of empties in from the Fowey branch to the 'down' goods loop. The locomotive was subsequently preserved by the National Railway Museum.

J. Vaughan

Plate 201 (Left): A tough load for a 'little'un'. Arriving at Lostwithiel in May 1976 with no less than 38 Clay Hoods is one of Laira's Class 25s, which were stabled at St. Blazey Depot. The small Bo-Bo locomotives were not particularly successful but they were regular china clay train performers from the early 1970s to the early 1980s. On the right is the former broad gauge goods shed which was demolished during 1983, preserved for re-erection at a later date, but subsequently burnt.

J. Vaughan

Plate 202 (Left): It is not often that the clay train operators have to cope with conditions like this. However this was the scene at Lostwithiel on 19th January 1985 when Cornwall experienced some heavy snowfalls. This line of clay wagons at Lostwithiel was photographed from a passing High Speed Train. Heavy rain, rather then snow, is the traditional enemy in Cornwall.

J. Vaughan

Plate 203: On 15th October 1982, one of the regular ECC customers had an urgent requirement for over 50 tonnes of china clay slurry. The need was so great that a special train was arranged, train crews alerted and the loading facility at Burngullow was prepared. Hauling the single Crossfield bogie tanker up to Treverrin Tunnel is 'Peak' No. 45015. This photograph was taken at 11.20 and four hours later the tanker was on its way back to Warrington with its precious cargo on board. The grazing sheep seem disinterested.

J. Vaughan

Plate 204: A delightfully mixed china clay ABS working passes Respryn Bridge, near the country estate of Lanhydrock, on 18th April 1985. Class 45/0 'Peak' No. 45069 heads three VDA Railfreight wagons, one PAA Tullis Russell wagon, four PRA vehicles, a bogie Crossfield slurry tanker, and three Traffic Services 80 tonne Polybulk wagons — about 720 tonnes gross — forming the 09.38 St. Blazey to Severn Tunnel Junction working.

J. Vaughan

Plate 205: From time to time a Class 37 interloper finds its way across the Royal Albert Bridge into Cornwall. Such was the case on 11th June 1986 when Immingham's No. 37104, with split headcode boxes, strayed into the Duchy. Rolling down past Treesmill with empty Clay Hoods, the Eastern Region invader was bound for Burngullow. During the summer of 1985 other ER Class 37s ended up at St. Blazey after they had worked a 'Saturdays Only' York to Penzance passenger relief.

J. Vaughan

Plate 206: On occasions, heavy china clay trains from St. Blazey to Lostwithiel are banked up the climb to Treverrin Tunnel, but at other times pairs of Class 37s have been used. Thundering out of Par on 18th April 1985 with forty Clay Hoods weighing some 800 tonnes and using all their 3,500hp output (less at the rail) are Nos. 37181 and 37247, as they make their way from Goonbarrow Junction to Carne Point, Fowey.

J. Vaughan

Plate 207: The two freights to Severn Tunnel Junction nearly always have Type 4 diesel power whereas the majority of local workings are with Type 3 locomotives. Although they are now being withdrawn, the Class 45/0s had, until 1st October 1985, been regular performers on the Severn Tunnel Junction workings, such as No. 45068 passing Treesmill with the 15.15 ex-St. Blazey of 29th February 1984.

J. Vaughan

Plate 208: Torrential rain at Par as the afternoon train from Parkandillack rolls in behind No. 37181. On this day, 20th April 1984, the train weighed 560 tonnes and included three German VTG Ferrywaggons and four 'Tigers'. The train will reverse at Par and be propelled round to St. Blazey Yard, where the load may be increased and a Type 4 locomotive will take over.

J. Vaughan

Plate 209: About to pass over the ornate road underpass at the popular Carlyon Bay golf course on 21st April 1983 is No. 47068 with just two ECC International 'Tiger' wagons. In the opposite direction the line climbs at a continuous 1 in 60 for most of the 4½ miles from Par to St. Austell. These wagons will be added to others at St. Blazey to form the afternoon ABS.

J. Vaughan

Plate 210: While colour lights have been replacing manual semaphore signals all over the BR system, at the time of writing, lower quadrant WR signals survive at Par. Sweeping off the main line and making for St. Blazey Yard at precisely 12.13 on 19th April 1985 is No. 45051 with the morning 'down' ABS from Severn Tunnel Junction. There are seven different types of clay-carrying wagon in the first eight vehicles, although all will empty at this stage.

J. Vaughan

Plate 211: From time to time one of the numerous 'freight' Class 47s is not available and a 'passenger' e.t.h. Class 47/4 is substituted. On this occasion the locals probably took a dim view of the substitute locomotive being No. 47602 *Glorious Devon,* an almost unacceptable sight on a Cornish branch line! The 'Duff' leaves the Drinnick Mill branch with a Burngullow to Carne Point working on 3rd October 1985.

J. Vaughan

CHINA CLAY MISCELLANY

Plate 212: As mentioned in the text, in the early months of 1986 trials were conducted with a former merry-go-round coal hopper as a potential replacement for the ageing Clay Hoods. A specially-cleaned HAA wagon, No. 351297, was provided and while a hood had not then been provided the hopper discharge system proved quite successful. By 1987 these wagons may start replacing the Clay Hoods thus providing a larger capacity payload with consequently fewer trains — and locomotive and manning economies. It is photographed at St. Blazey Yard in July 1986.

J. Vaughan

Plate 213: In the early 1980s, there was some discussion about the tendency of the successful but heavy Class 37s to wear out their wheel flanges on the tightly curved china clay sidings. Their 106 ton weight and Co-Co bogies were also causing problems with the track and there were rumours that Class 20s would be drafted in, but this never came to fruition. In this montage the author shows what might have been as a clay train leaves Lostwithiel. During 1986, Class 20s appeared in Cornwall for the first time — at the head of enthusiasts specials.

J. Vaughan

Plate 214: The author has always been fascinated by china clay trains, and on the night of 4th December 1976, in the capacity of one of the principals of Railway Pictorial Publications, organised the 'Western China Clay' Railtour. The tour took 600 passengers to Cornish branch lines for haulage by Class 52 locomotives. Just before departure at 00.30, No. D1023 *Western Fusilier* stands at Paddington Station before heading off into the night to the Duchy of Cornwall.

J. Vaughan

Plate 215: By July 1986 the new sub classes of Railfreight Class 37s had reached the West Country. Fresh from Crewe Works and in grey, black and yellow livery is No. 37696, posing in front of a calcified seaweed wagon and some crippled Clay Hoods at the rarely photographed Nanpean Wharf, near Drinnick Mill. In July 1986, the Clay Hood population had dwindled to 477 wagons, with only about 400 'runners'.

J. Vaughan

Plate 216: As mentioned in the caption for *Plate 213*, flange and track wear problems continued, and in 1986 a set of new 'self-steering bogies' were fitted to No. 37175. The bogies provided for more lateral movement on the axles, controlled by additional shock absorbers. In blue livery, with the large BR logo and 'Scottish Terrier' on its side, with Highland line style headlight mounting, the experimental locomotive is seen on a delightful train of one Clay Hood passing Treesmill on its way from Laira to St. Blazey, on 22nd July 1986.

J. Vaughan

Plate 217: Deep in the undergrowth something stirred! Only an annual visit from the weed killing train keeps some of the little used lines clear of vegetation but it is unlikely that the chemical reaches the far end of the Moorswater Sidings. With the driver hoping that there is still some sort of track beneath the long grass, No. 37207 creeps towards Coombe Junction with another load of clay which, while dried at Moorswater, has travelled by pipeline from Parsons Park on Bodmin Moor. 'Proper Job!'

J. Hicks

BIBLIOGRAPHY

Diesels in the Duchy — *John Vaughan* — Ian Allan — 1983
The Clay Hood — *Martin Pearce* — English China Clays — 1975
The History of English China Clays — *Kenneth Hudson* — David & Charles — 1969
The Story of Cornwall's Railways — *Anthony Fairclough* — Bradford Barton — 1970
The Bodmin and Wadebridge Railway — *C. F. D. Whetmath* — Town and Country Press — 1972
A History of the Cornish China Clay Industry — *R. M. Barton* — Bradford Barton — 1966
The Branch Lines of Cornwall — *Lewis Reade* — Atlantic Books — 1984
The Pentewan Railway — *Dr. M. J. T. Lewis* — Twelveheads Press — 1981
Caradon and Looe: Canal, Railways and Mines — *Michael J. Messenger* — Twelveheads Press — 1978
Diesels on Cornwall's Main Line — *H. L. Ford* — Bradford Barton — 1973
Cornwall's Railways (A Pictorial Survey) — *Anthony Fairclough* — Bradford Barton — 1972
The West Country (Regional History of Railways) — *David St. John Thomas* — David & Charles — 1981 Edition
The Cornish China Clay Traffic (Trains Illustrated Summer Annual) — *R. C. Riley* — Ian Allan — 1957
Treffrys Tramways — *the Late John Penderill-Church Ph.D.* — ECC International — 1979

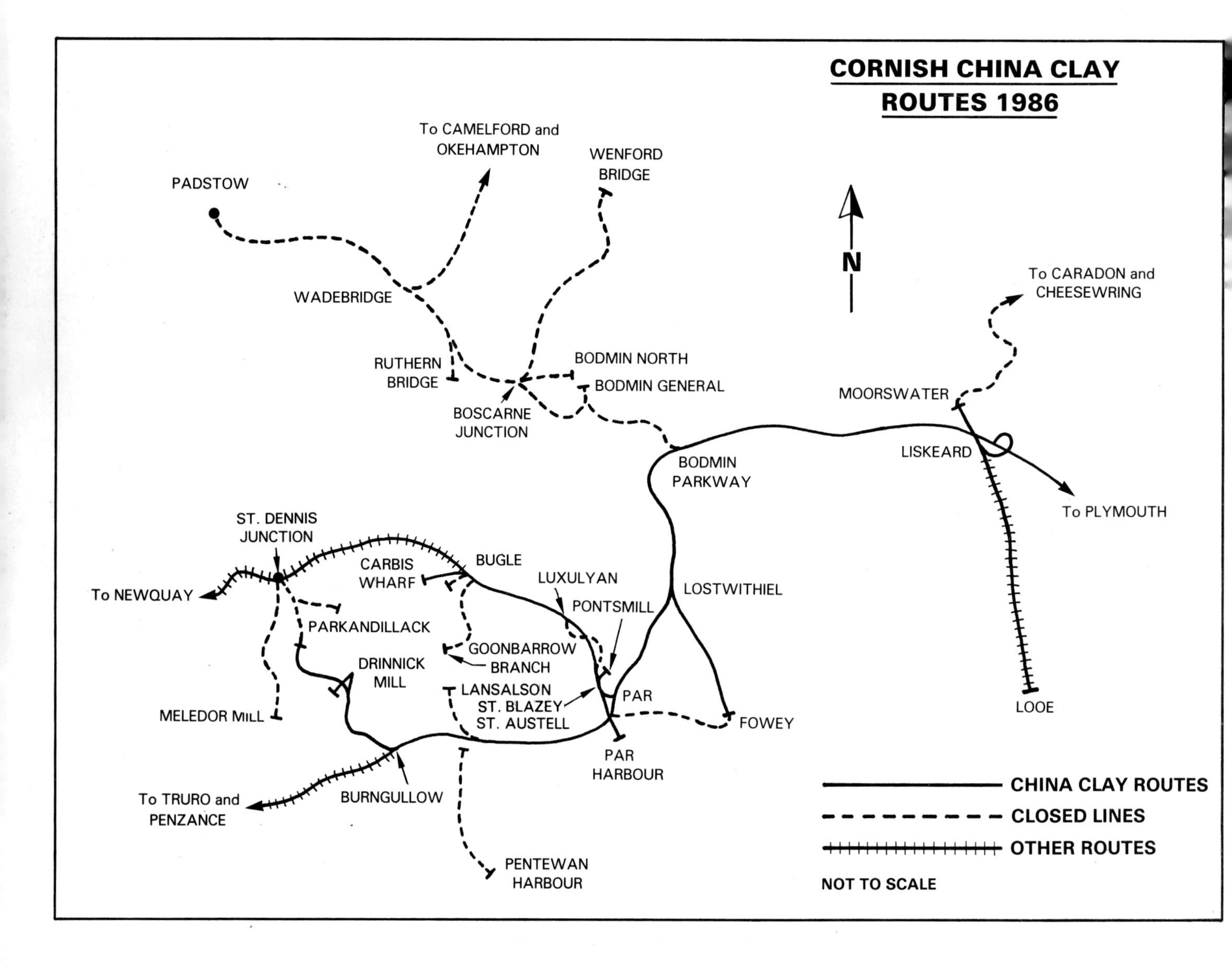